Living Through RELATIONSHIPS

Destiny or Freewill

Smita Mittal

BlueRose Publishers
New Delhi • London

First Published in August 2021

ISBN: 978-93-5472-384-1

BLUEROSE PUBLISHERS
www.bluerosepublishers.com
info@bluerosepublishers.com
+91 8882 898 898

Cover Design:
Muskan Sachdeva

Typographic Design:
Ilma Mirza

Distributed by: BlueRose, Amazon, Flipkart

AUTHOR'S NOTE

I am part of TLC, 'Teachers are Leaders', a Master Mind Circle. In this group a challenge of writing a book was thrown at us by the mentor of the group Guru Murali Sundaram. I took up the challenge and collected my ideas on a subject that is dear to me and which I felt forms the very foundation of our existence -Relationships. I thank Guru Murali for giving us this challenge as it opened a new avenue for me. My team of other master minds kept on pushing and applauding at every milestone reached. That really helped. Sachin Dahiya, VP of our Master Mind Circle, is a great motivator who along with Dr. Smita Malik encouraged me all the way. My grateful thanks to them.

I am very close to this topic, apart from it being my niche, I feel drawn by Relationships. In my life, all relationships are very dear to me. I always used to be fascinated by the way my parents used to maintain loving relationships with their siblings and friends. I could notice the difference how other people in the family would respond to their similar relatives. My parents had created a happy and vibrant home for us with a rich fabric of interwoven relationships. Their attitude of loving and supporting the immediate and extended family left a very deep impression on me. I started observing relationships and their impact, very early in life, as I grew up. Then my own life also presented various opportunities to observe and ponder over the dynamics of these relationships.

In my life I experienced that if, on one hand, relationships were my source of strength, happiness and relief; on the other hand, I suffered tremendous pain and agony also through relationships only. It made me think deeply about relationships. It made me wonder about what I had done to attract such persons in my life.

I had the good fortune of meeting and interacting with Swami Ram in Rishikesh and in Delhi too on and off from 1987 to 1994. Once I had asked him also and he had smiled and said 'Is it not a miracle that out of so many people here taking a walk by Ganga Barrage we two are talking. Think about it.' He gave me a hint, sort of nudged me on this path. Very learned swami of Ramakrishna Mission, Swami Vanishwaranand, lovingly called Dattu Maharaj also guided me on this path. Then much recently in the year 2019, I got the opportunity to interact with Guru ji Naushir and he answered my question that in human life destiny and freewill move hand in hand. That made me delve deeper into this subject. So when the opportunity came to me for writing a book, I chose this topic.

So many people helped me directly and indirectly. Mr. Ram Verma Sir is a very big and silent contributor in this book. I am his student and did 'Neuro Linguistic Programming and Re-imprinting of Subconscious' course with him. I will be forever indebted to him. My elder sister Mrs Renu Gupta is instrumental in putting me on the paths of NLP and TLC. Once I shared the idea of writing a book on this subject with my husband, Sanjay, he along with all the family members, encouraged me to write. My brilliant young niece, Neha, reviewed my work and provided insightful inputs.

Lastly, my publisher Blue Rose also helped in editing, polishing and presenting you the book in this form.

I truly believe that people come to us in their time to provide us the life experiences that we are destined to go through. Those experiences may be good or bad but we have to go through them as per our Karmic account. Just as in a train accident, all passengers are involved but each one goes through a different experience of relief, gratitude, fear, fright, hurt, deep wounds, amputations, or death!

While reading this book you will notice that most of the examples cited in it are from my life. I chose to share them with you for two reasons. First one is simple. They are my experiences; I did not have to take anyone's permission to cite them. Second and more importantly, I have gone through them, I know the feelings.

This book is about the relationships; the way I have deciphered them. All of us have the same relationships. All of us have parents, siblings, friends, spouses, children, in-laws etc. but all of us have different experiences. Because, in every relationship the people involved, have individual personalities with independent perceptions and reactions that give a very different tint to their relationships.

I have tried to cover as much as I could at that time. The topic is such that I kept on adding and editing. So if you want to discuss anything please feel free to reach me through my email:

smitamittal30@gmail.com

FOREWORD

Would you like to know the number one secret to long-term health?

A 75-year-old Harvard Medical School study confirms this.

"We are happier and healthier when we have good relationships."

They discovered that loneliness can kill people and that more socially connected people are healthier and happier.

In another study, they found out that a caring friend's support can offer some protection against the negative consequences of stress. Researchers discovered that participants who finished a demanding task performed better when they were reminded of people with whom they had great relationships.

It's not about the number of relationships we have, but about the quality of the ones we have with ourselves and others.

Relationships come in many forms. Relationships are hard to get, Easy to Ignore! Because of their perceived importance, people typically focus primarily on their work relationships than on their personal ones. Personal relationships, on the other hand, are the ones that keep us going throughout our lives.

Many people are aware that they should maintain cordial connections, yet they rarely do so. Relationships can only thrive when they are built on a solid foundation of truth. When a relationship fails, you must have the difficult conversation. It might not be pretty, and it might not feel pleasant. It will open up if you are willing to listen and tell the truth.

Your relationships will heal, connect, and thrive when you build them on truth and authenticity rather than masks, false perfection, and being phony. As a result, today is the ideal time to restore any broken connections in your life. Simply approach them and tell them the truth. The truth may be bitter but it is also a wonderful healer!

In this amazing book, Smita Mittal has given us excellent insights about relationships and how they find us, and how to navigate through them. This book is a beautiful note on how to find yourself through your relationships explained extremely well with Smita's own personal experiences and stories keeping the readers hooked. Healthy relationships can brighten our lives and bring out the best in people I am extremely proud of our TLC Helios member for releasing her first book to help as many people as possible.

Murali Sundaram

Happyness coach

Founder- TLC Masterminds

(www.teachersareleaders.org)

PREFACE

'Relationships are more important than life, but it is important for those relationships have life in them.'

~ Swami Vivekananda

What are relationships...? How are they formed...? How do they develop...?

The definition of 'relationship' in *English Language Learners Dictionary* states, 'The way two or more people, groups, countries, etc., talk to, behave towards, and deal with each other and are connected.' But do we just want to relate or do we want to relate meaningfully? Our relationship may be formal or close, a long or short one, but it can be meaningful. Meaningful relationships provide the opportunity for three key benefits: exchange of support, social engagement, and sense of worth, which are the major pillars for the foundation of healthy ageing.

Looking seriously and deeply into your relationships, you will realize that relationships find you—you just live them. We get our very first taste of relationships—our parents—through no personal effort! In the same way, we get our siblings and extended family and mind you, every one of them leaves a mark on our personality. We are born into a family. Likewise, we find our friends, or our friendships find us! We make friends because we feel comfortable with them but many a time we don't agree with a lot of things that our friends do. Still, we keep the friendships going and learn to enjoy them!

As we grow, a time comes to find the most important relationship of our life: a life partner. For some of us, our parents decide that it is time for us to settle down and they start looking for our life partner. Their search is restricted by many filters: caste, family, status, etc. But still, they zero in on one family after all the inquiry and background research. They leave no stone unturned to marry us off with great love, care, blessings and pomp. However, sometimes the future doesn't unfold as everyone had anticipated. We suffer and with us, they suffer too. Why? When everything was looked into, every step was taken with the concerned party's concurrence, then where was the scope for friction or failure? But friction and misunderstandings do take place in relationships and then trouble starts brewing in paradise.

In another scenario, someone, somewhere, decides to settle down and starts looking for a partner. You, a complete stranger, comes into that person's orbit and the two of you come together. But why do only you come together? There are so many boys and girls around; why don't you just fall for anyone? What is so special about that one particular person that makes you think 'Yes! This is the one!'? What is it that you are searching for? Obviously, it is something that only you know, only you can feel, as no one else can see it! You fall for the person. You fall so hard that you are willing to defy your family, the society, or anyone who stands in your way, for this relationship. You want to marry the person with or without the blessings of your family or society. If you are blessed, you live your life happily with your chosen one. But many times you start wondering about your own choice once the euphoria settles down. You start noticing the basic differences in their value system, daily habits, temperaments, or even in basic personalities that you can get to know only after living together under the same roof as husband and wife. You try to maintain the relationship and continue. But sometimes it becomes difficult and you decide to part ways. To come out of this relationship is not easy, mentally and emotionally it puts you in a wringer, but still you decide to take this step. After coming out of this relationship, you feel free. So, again the question comes up: are relationships made by you or maintained by you? You exercised your free will in the hope of finding eternal happiness by selecting your own partner, but destiny had something else in store for you.

I have seen the same thing happening many times in career/job selections/professional relations too. So when you are looking for something else, you land up with something completely unexpected. I will share my life experience.

I was raised to be a good housewife, and I was very happy and satisfied taking care of my home and child. While helping my young child with his homework, I was noticing careless correction oversights by a certain subject teacher. I tried to correct my son but he just wouldn't listen to me stating that the teacher knows better. You know how these young children almost worship their teachers. Their relationship with their teacher is full of trust and admiration. Now the question in front of me was, what do I do? I didn't want to say anything against his teacher and at the same time didn't want him to learn wrong things either. So, I went to the principal with an appointment and the evidence. The principal was taken aback and assured me that she would look into the matter. Before I could reach home, a school clerk was waiting at my house with a letter. With a lot of trepidation, I opened the envelop, dreading the worst. But to my utter shock, it was an offer to join the school as a staff member. To get an offer from such a reputed school was beyond my dreams, especially when I do not hold any professional teaching degree! I didn't know what to say. I asked for some time and after consulting with my husband I accepted the offer. How will you define it? Destiny definitely presented the door and then, with my free will, I opened it! Destiny offered an opportunity to develop a good relationship with a reputed organization and with my free will I accepted it and went on to become the principal of an IB school, still without a professional degree!

Another example from life: after we returned to India, my husband had three fantastic job offers in his hand. After lot of considerations and meetings, he signed with one company, feeling that this is where he would retire from. But destiny had something else in store for us and this budding relationship between him and the company. Very soon my husband was looking for a way out. In this case, free will was exercised and then destiny took over. If you understand these points then it will be easy for you to live through this life and the relationships in it peacefully.

In all our relationships, whether personal, social or official, we just walk into them or we receive them and then keep on trying to make some sense out of them. We all are destined to go through certain experiences in life; some good and some bad, based on our karmic account. To settle these accounts, we have to go through certain situations brought together through our relationships. We attract people and situations accordingly. In life and in relationships, our destiny and our free will work together. Sometimes we meet a person or are placed in a situation through no effort of ours, going through an experience that we had never foreseen.

There are certain things that are under our control: how to manage our time, how to manage people and relationships, how to acquire and hone skills, etc. But what results we will get out of them is not in our hands. Sometimes a little effort yields amazing results but sometimes even sincere hard work is not able to produce results close to our expectations. Some people enjoy very good relationships seemingly without making much effort, yet there are people who, despite their desire and keenness, are not able to retain or maintain happy relationships.

Our relationships become the medium for karmic experiences. Hence, it is fundamental to know how to handle, develop, and retain the relationships that we have. In this book, we will deal with these issues and try to understand them.

Table of Content

Chapter One

Mystic Antenna

'Man can do what he wills but he cannot will what he wills.'

~ Arthur Schopenhauer

(A German philosopher known for his work The World as Will and Representation, 1818)

Humans are wrapped in relationships, always attracting or getting attracted to people known or unknown. In the next two chapters we will discuss this and why people come into our lives. What attracts them?

Human life is the sum total of its relationships; relationship with family, friends, career, society, beliefs: intellectual or spiritual and self. You are born into a family. You have no control over it. The only control you can exercise is that the kind of personal equations you develop with your family's individual members. Sometimes even that seems to be out of your control. We will discuss that in a later chapter.

First, let us understand how and why people come into your life. We will divide it in two parts. We will deal with first aspect, free will, in this chapter and the second aspect, destiny, in the next chapter 'Cosmic Intervention'.

You are like a transmitter, sending and receiving signals consciously and subconsciously all the time. Human beings are part of the cosmic energy, and what we speak or think creates waves and sends signal out in the universe. You can call it the Law of Attraction too. It is like gravity—it is always in effect and always active.

When you focus on something, you believe in something, you get that. Your internal belief and your unquestioning faith attracts that into your orbit. You will get whatever you will focus your energy and attention on. This works all the time in your lives and the people you attract in it. If you are positive, then you will attract positive people and if you are unsure, nervous or negative then that is the kind of people you will encounter in your life. Whatever you think or feel is your way of requesting the universe to give you more of the same.

'Once you make a decision, the universe conspires to make it happen.'

~ Ralph Waldo Emerson

(Mostly known by his middle name Waldo, he was an American essayist, lecturer, philosopher and poet)

This' Law of Attraction' becomes very clear in your relationships. Based on your own beliefs and emotions, you attract people in your orbit and develop your relationships with them. Life is very intricately woven with relationships; relationships with others and, more importantly, relationship with self. Yes, with yourself! You see, this is your life. All the achievements, all the failures, all the relations, all connections are yours. You have attracted them and you are keeping them and maintaining them by the force of your personality. Your personality acts like a glue to your relationships. Yes, I agree, some of those relations you have inherited while some of them you are forced to maintain due to personal/ social/ professional obligations. But there are some with whom you connect on a personal level. What kind of a relationship do you have with them? Is it smooth or is it tumultuous? Is it an on-again-off-again kind of relationship? If the condition is like this, then you need to introspect. People relate to you and your personality. If the two do not match, then it confuses the people and it becomes difficult for them to develop a long-lasting relationship.

You are the magnet that is keeping your family, friends, colleagues and acquaintances together. Obviously, you would like to be a strong magnet. Your magnetic quality depends on how you see yourself. If you yourself are clear with the kind of person you are then all your thoughts, statements and actions will match the image you carry of yourself in your mind. It is very important to know and understand yourself, and to have a good relationship with yourself.

You will appreciate that you are the only common link in all your relationships. You can keep them coherent only if your behaviour is consistent. See, to convey anything clearly you should have clarity in your mind about it. In relationships, people get connected to the person that you are. And if you are not clear, or are confused, obviously you will give confusing signals in your relationships without realizing. Your relations will also remain confused. Some might just drift away or become disinterested. Then you will worry, will feel disappointed, or feel sad and angry that people don't understand you.

When you are not clear in your mind, you are not able to think clearly. You are not sure what you want from your life or your relationships. Hence, you keep on drifting without any clear direction. You become like a rudderless boat that keeps on moving at the mercy of the sea current. In this situation, you are not able to send or receive any strong signal in the universe. The people you attract are also like you, who are not clear of what they want in life. So you end up having weak and temporary relationships that play on your mind; life becomes miserable.

You may be a nice person, but if you are not a clear-minded person your relationships will always suffer. Due to this lack of clarity in mind, your opinions, your beliefs, and your views will get affected. Your statements will also change, your reactions and responses will change, and so will change your likes and dislikes. All this is bound to have an adverse effect on people around you as it will leave them baffled! Anyone can adjust and accommodate up to a point but beyond a certain point it becomes next to impossible. Your lamentation that it is your life and you have the right to change your opinion will not be of any use!

But if you understand yourself, if you are clear in what you want from life, then your actions will be clearly focused in that direction. Because of this clarity, your thoughts will also be more focused and you will be able to attract better people in your orbit. When you are strong and you are attracting stronger people in your life, life itself becomes smoother and happier. This opens the pathways for better relationships. Remember that there is abundance in the universe. You get what you work for and believe in.

When you know yourself, you will know your priorities, your goals, and your aspirations—in relationships and in life. Once these are clear in your mind, you will begin looking for friends who will help and support you in fulfilling the newfound priorities. When your friends are on the same page as you are, you will have better relationships with them. The main reason for this will be that you would like to spend more time together as there will be so much to share. Even the disagreements will be different; there will be differences of opinions but not differences in values. Differences of opinions in any relationship are bound to happen as you both are intelligent and independent. Because you value the person and respect his intelligence, you will be able to take it in your stride and the matter will end there. But if there is difference in values, then the patch-up becomes difficult as the whole approach is very different then. Values are the basis of our belief system, which become the basis for our intentions, which in turn generate our thoughts and motivate us to take action.

Another benefit of accepting yourself is that you end up knowing and realizing your weaknesses too. Once you are familiar with them, you can work upon them or look for friends and partners that can compensate for them. This way your team will always be strong. If you enter the arena without knowing your weak spots, you will always be exposed for exploitation. I will share with you my example. I am a little impulsive. Sometimes I take very quick decisions but my husband is very grounded. He knows me very well. So, in situations where he knows that I might take a decision that I might regret later, he remains with me and takes the lead. This way we make a good team.

When you know yourself, the clarity that comes in your thinking and behaviour is beneficial for your relationships as well. People around you know what you want and what to expect from you. Yes, it becomes a little predictable but then this predictability is not boring; instead, it is reliable. It makes you more trustworthy and believable. These two qualities are very strong magnets. In your life, also, you must have noticed that people like to have stronger relationships with people who are more reliable. They may hang out with everyone but when it comes to having serious friendships or relationships, they look for these qualities.

In the reverse scenario, if you don't know yourself, how can others know you? It will be next to impossible for them to understand you. If you keep sending mixed signals depending on your mood or your shifting desires, there will be nothing but confusion in your relationships. Relationships are built on consistency. Based on desires, you may enjoy a short-term relationship or friendship. You can't have a long-term relationship based on moods, whims or fancies. The consistency of your interactions, responses, reactions, behaviour, and emotional stability contributes to your relationships, and all this depends on your mental state and attitude.

It also depends on what you want from your relationships. Where do you place them in your life? What future have you set for them? How far are you willing to go to maintain them and keep them in your life? You can answer all these questions only if you have searched for them within. You have to spend time with yourself. You have to set priorities for yourself. Hence, the kind of relationship you enjoy with yourself is very important. It reflects in the decisions you take in your life, the goals you set for yourself or the picture you see for your future, and the way you present yourself in front of people.

When you understand yourself, you present yourself as a confident, cheerful, enigmatic, and reliable person. When you have not tried to understand or analyse your feelings or your emotions, you will come across as confused, easy-going, adjustable, and a happy-go-lucky kind of person because your attitude will be to 'let it be this time, I will check it next time' or 'I am not sure what stand to take'. These are not definitely negative qualities but they do not inspire confidence in others either. All put together, do not .it portrays the personality that may not stand up for personal rights. Appeasement is not always a good strategy in relationships. I can say so with conviction from my experiences.

If there are many things that you don't like about yourself but are doing nothing to rectify them, then you will be full of anger with very little patience. Aggression will become your defence mechanism and you will not even realize when it has become your personality. The same is with the case of liking yourself too much. This will make you too proud and very soon you will start having a superiority complex, which hinders your growth. So always be vigilant to avoid developing any complex, be it superior or inferior.

When you are happy with yourself, you exude confidence but when you are not happy with yourself, it shows in your body language and the way you interact with others. Because of the way you see yourselves, people notice and their behaviour and reactions towards you also changes, moulding your relationships with them accordingly.

As we already have discussed, all of us are receivers and transmitters, constantly sending and receiving signals. Your mind starts attracting those kinds of people and opportunities for you which you are concentrating on consciously or subconsciously. You are living in a society surrounded by people and interacting with them constantly in verbal or non-verbal form. When you interact, you not only exchange word or looks, you also exchange vibes at a very subconscious level. That is why you must have noticed that, sometimes, you just click with a total stranger. This is because of the matching vibes at that time! Through your interactions, you send vibrations and these vibrations attract people. You must have experienced that in a big gathering of strangers too, when you notice only few people and vice versa. Why? In that big gathering, also, you are able to attract some like-minded people. Is it not strange? The same principal applies here too. When you sincerely trust in some dream, it fructifies. You meet those supportive people, you are able to turn adverse situations into favourable ones, and you realize your dream. But for that you have to have trust; just belief will not take you far.

There is a very interesting story that explains the difference between belief and trust beautifully. It goes like this: one day, people noticed a man walking between two high-rise buildings on a tight rope with his very young daughter sitting calmly on his shoulders. He was swaying because of the wind. Viewers had gathered down below with bated breath. But both father and daughter kept their cool and walked the rope successfully. Once they crossed, viewers broke into spontaneous applause. Everyone was impressed. The father came down with his daughter and joined the crowd. Then he set up two high tripods and tied a rope across them. He asked the crowd whether it believed that he will be able to walk across the rope on the tripods. Everyone said yes because they believed in him. If he could do it so high above between the buildings then this walk is going to be a cake walk for him. Now the father asked the audience who would like his child to sit on his shoulders this time. No one came forward. This is the difference between belief and trust! His daughter trusted him! You need to trust yourself.

We all visualize our future of healthy relationships. Some dreams you visualize consciously and some play in your subconscious all the time. These are the dreams you should be aware of. Because, whether you are aware or not, your mind is constantly sending signals based on these subconscious dreams and you end up attracting those situations and those participants. So many times I have met people who are building big projects or getting into major relationships, but they are thinking of failures all the time and ultimately they fail because they have no trust in the project or relationship. Their mind didn't give it a chance to survive. On the other hand, I have seen some exponential career growths and very successful relationships too. The mind attracts the vibrations and responds to them. Everything is available in abundance in this universe.

To give your relationships a solid base, you should have a good understanding of yourself. Let me explain it further. Everybody has different expectations from life and in turn from self. So the benchmarks are always different for different individuals. Here, we are not discussing the standard of benchmark one should set for oneself. I am just stating that as long as you are meeting your set expectations from your-self, you will be satisfied. When you are satisfied with yourself, you are confident, settled, and calm. Even if you come across some unexpected or unpleasant situation, you will be able to handle it calmly and retain your cool.

On the other hand, when you are not happy with yourself for whatever reason—be it looks, qualification, background, intelligence or any other factual or imaginary thing—you constantly feel inadequate, less capable and less confident. In this mental state, whenever you come across any challenging person or situation, you give in easily but continue to feel bad about it. It becomes a spiral and it does not help anyone, least of all you.

It is very important to know yourself and accept yourself the way you are, with all the flaws and strengths. Once you accept it, that means you have analysed yourself and acknowledge the areas to nurture and nourish. Mind you, it is not an easy exercise. You are your biggest critique. So many times, I have come across people suffering from past guilt of misbehaviour, missed opportunities, misconceptions, misunderstandings. This feeling of guilt keeps them nailed in that particular time zone and does not allow them to move forward. Even though they feel guilty, they do not do anything to correct it either. Their false ego does not allow them to seek forgiveness from the hurt party! If only they had gathered the courage and taken this step, they could have saved themselves from a lot of heart burn!

Seeking forgiveness from others requires courage but forgiving yourself requires large-heartedness. Because, in your heart of hearts, you know the petty reasons for which you did not do the right thing. This has far-reaching effects on relationships. To accept this even to yourself is not easy. I would like to share one very telling experience here. I was a class teacher of grade VI. I used to make it a point to connect individually with all my students. It would allow me to help them through their lives' stumbling blocks. I began noticing continued restlessness in one of my students who was usually quiet and stayed aloof. I asked him the reason and suggested that he can talk to me whenever he is ready. After a few days, he asked me if we can talk. Of course, I agreed and we went for a round in the playground. There, during that walk in the dusty field, he mumbled that he is being molested by his cousin and no one in the family believes him. Just imagine the mental state of a 12-year-old boy, all alone in the midst of his family and totally insecure at home. Both the things that we rely upon had betrayed him. I was shocked!

The school called his parents, but they were too busy. His grandfather agreed to come and after listening to the story he started crying bitterly. He said that he had lost two grandsons in one day. One who was a victim of not only the rapist but the whole family's distrust, and other who was the tormentor. His guilt was so strong that we had to counsel him too. He was not able to forgive himself for doubting his younger grandson only because his older grandson used to bring good grades. This one sitting had shaken his value system. But then he took control of the situation and brought his elder grandson also for counselling. Remember, as long as your mistake was not morally or legally wrong, you should try to forgive yourself after learning your lesson from it and move ahead. Every relationship involves communication; listening and trust are especially important to keeping the relationship healthy and growing.

Self-acceptance and forgiveness are two very important steps for self-growth. You are a mirror that needs to be polished constantly. You cannot sit on your past laurels. You have to keep working on yourself to find the best in you. Every peak is a step upwards in the ladder of life. You are always a work in progress. With the passing of time, you grow, gain more experiences, gather more impressions, but so does your surrounding environment! You are constantly learning, adjusting, and adapting to your environment. Keep in mind, just as you are getting affected with this quickly changing environment, so are others. Everyone is doing exactly what you are doing but at a different pace and from a different perspective. Your relationships are always evolving. Be willing to accept these finer changes.

Now we know how we attract people in our lives with our free will, which is based on our beliefs and thoughts. We have also read that with our free will, based on our personality, we develop relationships— some already exist and some we find. Every person you encounter comes in your life for a reason. All the important people who leave a mark in your life are there to settle karmic debts. They are destined to be in your life at the particular moment for a particular purpose. They serve that purpose, settle the debt, and go away. We will discuss this in the next chapter 'Cosmic Interventions'.

Chapter Two

Cosmic Intervention

'Life is like a game of cards. The hand you are dealt is determinism; the way you play it is free will.'

~ Jawaharlal Nehru
(First Indian Prime Minister)

Relationships are based on experiences, memories, and beliefs. The kind of emotions you have experienced with the person helps you in deciding what kind of relationship you would like to have. Memories also play a very important role in the development of relationships. Every meeting with a person, every interaction, look, and gesture exchanged, is noticed and recorded by brain cells. All of these help in creating impressions. And these impressions create our memories. Based on these memories, we develop the bonding in a relationship (we will be discussing this in detail in the next chapter). But then there are exceptions too. There must be members in your family itself whom you meet on a regular basis but still don't feel any warmth towards, but there must be a few whom you meet rarely but you remember them fondly and want to meet again. If anyone asks you to explain, you may not be able to give the justification but the fact remains. In this chapter, we will focus on such relationships.

Sometimes you bump into a total stranger, feel an instant connection, and develop a good friendship. Why? What attracted both of you to each other? You may not be able to answer, but the fact is that you developed a good friendship, and that connection remains till it serves a purpose. This indicates that the two of you were destined to meet. That purpose can be big or small, or it may be completely emotional too. Once, I had gone to a plant nursery to buy some plants. There was another, quite senior couple also selecting plants. We started talking and immediately felt a comfort level that only very old friends feel. We remained good friends till the old lady passed away and I felt a vacuum after her departure. Had you looked at us as a pair, there was no match. She was much senior in age, had a very different background and financial status, but all these things never came in the way of our friendship! We would talk at length whenever we could connect. She would share her intimate emotions with me and I would quietly listen to her. She would pour her heart out to me and feel lighter. It was as if we were destined to be friends for that period of time and fulfil our emotional obligations to each other.

There is this explanation that rings true to me. Many of your relationships are there in your life to help you clear your debt of karmas or make your life richer. Let us look at the relationships from this angle too. Every person who comes in your life comes for a purpose. It is predefined. What you learn from him/her is your will. How you handle that learning is also your free will. Whether you learn, tolerate, ignore, revolt, pacify, adjust, mould, build, or break, it all depends on you. Just remember that this will not be the only experience; there will be more to come.

This is easier to understand for the followers of Hindu philosophy as believers in karmic cycles and rebirths. Hindu philosophy says that all human beings are part of one Supreme Being. All are one soul, and the soul comes to earth to complete its karmic cycle and attain Moksha or Nirvana (Salvation). To help it achieve this, other souls support it by providing certain situations through which this soul can settle its debts of karma.

All of us accumulate a mixed bag of good and bad karma in our lives on earth, living through relationships. We hurt some people, we please some people. When the soul leaves the body, it is free of the bondages of the body but not of the debts it has accumulated during its sojourn on earth. To be able to complete its journey, the soul has to clear all the debts. To do so, it has to come back and that is when it seeks the help of other connected souls to clean its slate of pending accounts. Hence, it is predestined where the soul will take birth, who will be its family members and what role will they play in its journey, who all will come in contact with it and what experiences will they provide this soul to settle the accounts. This way, all the relations are predestined, all the experiences are also predestined. The only thing in your control is how you respond to these relations and experiences. Do you succeed in clearing your debt or do you end up adding to your already existing list of them?

If you look at relationships from this angle then the whole perspective changes. Then it means that relations that are giving you happiness are fulfilling their karma. You should accept it gracefully without hurting them to avoid collecting any negative karma. By gracefully, I mean without resistance. If someone is doing you a good deed without being asked or prompted, then accept it in the same spirit. When things are are going the way you had desired or you are reaping results as per your plan, you should remember to be grateful to the people who have helped you reach your goal. If at this time you allow your ego to become bigger than your self- respect, then you will add negative karma to your list.

In the same light, people who are giving you pain or creating hurdles in your path are providing you with the opportunity to live out your karmic cycle. You had hurt many people knowingly or unknowingly in your past life and must have had caused pain to them. Now is the time to go through the similar pain to learn the impact your words and actions can have on others. You should be grateful for their help in fulfilling your obligations instead of getting irritated. Because if you get irritated then you will be accumulating more and more obligations and will be mired in them! That is why it is important to be grateful all the time. Count your blessings for the opportunities to cleanse your slate through various relationships that have surrounded you. With your free will you can help your destiny or you can create road blocks and cause hindrance.

Now, you can raise the argument that, going by this philosophy, you should continue to suffer as maybe that is your destiny! But this will be a misinterpretation of this theory. When it says that people are in your life to give you certain experiences, it doesn't encourage exploitation. Of course, if you are harassed, tortured, wronged or hurt, you must stand up against that. You must fight for your dignity and self-respect. When people get murdered, or brides get burnt, or girls get raped, it is definitely not their destiny. It is the result of unchecked free will, unbridled emotions, and untamed ego. As C. S. Lewis says, 'Evil comes from the abuse of free will'. We enjoy the fruits of good karma and face the consequences of our wrong doings too. So, when you draw the line against suffering, then, in a way, you would be helping your tormentor by stopping him from accumulating his bad karma.

Living through the relationships with this belief can make the journey a little easier. This philosophy says that when the time comes for the soul to take birth on earth based on its karma, other souls also come on earth to fulfil their obligations. As a connected chain, every soul goes through its own obligation while helping the other souls to do the same. Since the roles of the souls in the life on earth are predefined, you take birth in a family that is pre-decided for you. You get a set of parents and with them an environment too. Your siblings also come along and so does your extended family. You learn from them and their environment. What you learn is your free will and the kind of relationships you develop depends on your free will too.

You must have noticed that despite having the same parents, same environment, same facilities and same problems, siblings have very different personalities. It is because what they chose to see and take from their environment. It is partly their destiny and partly free will. As you grow, you become a little selective of people. You pay more attention to the company that you join. But, despite all the caution and due diligence, do things always go as you had envisaged? Do you experience what you had set out for? This question stands for your friendships, relationships and your job too.

So many times it happens that, despite all the background work, you end up in a very different situation than you had anticipated. Take, for example, the selection of your life partner. I have seen people getting married to a person who is not at all like the one they were looking for. But it seems when the destined person comes in front of them, all the parameters are forgotten and that person becomes the centre of their life! I know of a person who is very well-educated, stylish and a suave gentleman. He had rejected a lot of proposals as his bar of expectation was very high. We used to wonder about the kind of girl he would say 'yes' to. So when we heard that he is getting married, there was a buzz. Everyone was curious to see his bride! After his arrival he threw a party to introduce his bride to everyone. All of us were surprised to meet her. She was a sweet person but not the kind that he always used to claim his wife would be. Honestly speaking, initially all of us were disappointed but later on, as we saw the genuine love and respect and care between them, we all were also content. Later on, he shared that after meeting her, he couldn't think of anyone else. It was as if he had met his soulmate, and that was all that mattered. We remained in touch with them for almost 15 years and they were totally mismatched and yet completely in love with each other.

On the other hand, one marries with full commitment and love, dreaming of a long and happy life together with one's partner. That person is committed to the relationship. Initially everything goes as he had dreamt, but gradually things start taking a wrong turn. Both of them are good people, both of them want the relationship, but personal differences keep on piling up. Or one of them starts drifting away. One feels saddened, while the other feels disappointed. The reality is that one was destined to go through the pleasures and the pains with that soul for a certain time. Once that account was over, the connection also served its purpose and one had to move on.

People come and go in your life, situations develop and unfold in their own sweet time, and the only thing in your control is how you handle it and what you take from it. That is your free will, which you are free to exercise and you do so, too. For example, one person was living his routine, middle-class life. One day, while going to office, he bumped into his childhood friend who had gone away and now was visiting this place again after earning a lot of wealth. He wanted to put up a plant and needed a reliable person. Both of them started talking and the friend made the offer to make this person in-charge of that plant. Within two hours, this person's life changed for the better. This is how destiny works. Now fast forward over a few years, and he becomes over-confident, taking everything for granted. He started feeling that he is the one who is responsible for all the success, became lax and started taking decisions based on his desire, not merit. Very soon his downfall began and he almost reached where he had begun. That is the impact of free will.

No situation is unique. No relationship is unique. Your perception of it makes it unique. Each human being has a very unique perception ability. (We will discuss how we perceive things in the next chapter.) No two human beings will react to the same situation in the same way. Their personality, their emotional intelligence, and their belief system lend a very unique mix to their perception. Their response to the people or situation is their free will. That's why, though the name of the relationship is the same for everyone, the people who are in it experience it in a very different way.

Stay away from the delusional game of 'Blame and Claim', where you start feeling self-important and claiming personal achievements when circumstances are favourable, or you start blaming others when tables are turned. As the outcomes are already decided, the game is just the reflection of your ego. It comes into play when you start believing that things are happening because of you, that you are the cause that is impacting the lives of people. This is the time to take stock of your actions. This is the time to introspect and realize the truth. These things are not in your control. Had they been, none of your relationships would have ever failed or you would never have suffered from sorrow. You cannot change your destiny but you can definitely change the intensity of its impact through the conscious practice of free will.

To clear the debt of karma, it is important to remember not to add the new to the already existing list. The only way to do that is told in the Bhagavad Gita. It says that one has to be sthir pragya, that is one has to remain stable in mind (sthir means stable and pragya means intellect). What is 'Stability in Mind'? It is not being affected by your surroundings; not to allow your thinking to get coloured by your emotions or get impressed by the emotional environment of the situation, and being able to see the situation and person in a detached, objective manner. Now, that is a tall order! When you are going through emotional roller coaster in your relationship, it is not easy to remain calm. It comes naturally to react: celebrate in happiness or wallow in sadness. But this is where you can change the game; practice taking happiness with humility and pain with gratitude. Just remember that pain or pleasure is just the by-product of settling your karmic accounts here. If you are able to remember this, even to some percentage, you can overcome a lot of problems in relationships and life.

If you ask is it possible to live like this, then I will say YES—though it is definitely not easy. But this is the only way to live through such relationships if you want peace of mind. Here I would like to share another very personal example from my own life. Like many young brides, I also have suffered because of problems with my in-laws and the toxicity of this relationship. I suffered for years till I started looking at the situation with the new lenses of the karmic cycle! Once I did this, my whole perspective changed. The situation remained the same but my response to it was very different. It stopped impacting me emotionally. I learnt to look at the bigger picture. I went through all the pain with the realization that I have to go through it to cleanse my soul of bad karma, but I took away the power and the satisfaction the person was holding over me. I learnt to be grateful for the solid support of my husband, my young son, and extended family and friends. I acknowledged that if on one hand I had to deal with that toxicity, I had the pleasure of being surrounded by so much of support and positivity. It helped me to focus on positivity. Peace came to my mind, and my health improved.

When I say this, please note that I do not mean that you take abuse quietly, believing that it is your destiny. You have not come to earth to take abuse or to abuse your fellow beings. You are carrying a reflection of God in you! You have come to earth to realize your goal, contribute in the general well-being of your relationships and the people you are surrounded with. Live your life peacefully and let others live theirs. You are here to learn from others and help others to learn from you, to expand your horizons, for self- realization! If anyone threatens you it is your legal, moral, and spiritual right to stop the person. Yes, you have to go through positive and negative experiences, you have to pass through tough situations in your life and relationships, but no one has the right to push you to the brink or try to break you emotionally, mentally, psychologically or spiritually. Look at your situation carefully and make your decision carefully; protect your rights without impinging on others while doing so.

You can do so in relationships by setting boundaries You see, every relationship has its scope and limits. If you know that, it will help you and others to not to cross that. Yes, you might have certain relationships that you cannot do anything about. Due to various reasons, you have to carry them along, but if you know that you have to keep them in your life, then be clear about the extent of their limits as well. It will bring balance in the relationship.

Relationships are there in life to make you move forward. They act to motivate, support, share and contribute, to cherish and make you grow. At every step of life, at every new turn, new relations come into your sphere of life to serve their purpose. You must see them as they are. Be grateful that they have connected with you for as long as they are there. Try to remain detached while connecting with people to contribute in their lives. There is a beautiful saying: 'Detachment is not that you should own nothing, but it is that nothing should own you.'

In the next chapter, we will discuss how these relationships develop, what is the basis for them, and, most importantly, how the mind and the belief system impact all relationships in life.

Chapter Three

Mosaic of Memories and Perceptions

'The meeting of two personalities is like the contact of two chemical substances: if there is any reaction, both are transformed.'

~ C. G. Jung

(Carl Gustav Jung, a Swiss psychiatrist whose work has been influential in many fields)

Life is a mosaic of memories: memories of relationships, memories of events, memories of the impressions and of conduct; yours and others too. How these memories are formed in your unfathomable mind is interesting. Memories are formed based on your perception of the event or the person. Your perception is your truth about the event or the person. The way you perceive the situation, event, or person is unique to you. It is your reality and your truth! That is what you believe, and on that basis itself you plan your next step or strategy and form your relationships.

Your brain is like a computer. It is a huge storage house. And like any computer it also has a language, and a method to decipher all the events and store all the memories. Your brain has around 80 billion neurons to store your memories. These 80 billions cells are interacting with each other all the time. Whatever happens in your body, the brain receives the signal and sends it back with the appropriate command almost instantaneously. It has a long history to fall back upon for these auto responses that are passed through genes, generation to generation. Like, when hungry, you look for food; when you perceive danger, you know you should fight or flight, you are more alert in dark; as show of affection, you hug, etc. These responses come naturally to you as your brain has already developed neural pathways to handle these situations.

The mind behaves in a totally different way than the brain. Here, the response is not auto generated. It is not that what you see or hear gets registered just like that in your mind too. No, not at all! It is your memory of the event and the person that does, so your personality, preferences, and past experiences play a major role in forming a memory. It all happens so smoothly and so quickly that you don't even realize it. The mind is a powerful tool that God has gifted to you. You don't even realize how your mind manipulates your relationships. For example, you think that Google is a tool that you are using and you go there to search for something you are looking for. Google presents in front of you the data with some advertisements based on your past preferences and searches. So your research is not as unbiased as you think it is.

Your mind also does the same to you and your relationship. If you like a person, your mind will bring forward all the actions, behaviour, looks, and conversations, reactions that you had liked. In the same way, if you don't like someone then the mind will present all the points you dislike about him. Before your conscious mind, your subconscious mind forms an opinion about the person and influences you. That is how you fall in love at first sight!

The mind has three filters through which all our sensory receptions go through. Whatever we see, hear, smell, taste or feel goes through these filters. Every event that you witness has to pass the filters. These three filters are interlinked and yet independent. Here, I would not get into the functions of the brain but focus on how our mind works. Each filter plays a very important role in developing a memory. Keep in mind that these filters have no physiological manifestation; they are purely the functioning of a mind and they play a very important role in forming all your relationships.

The first filter is Deletion. When you see, hear, or experience any event or meeting, your mind automatically deletes the points/parts it knows you will not need. This decision is made based on your past preferences. It follows an algorithm, just like

Google or Facebook that put forward advertisements based on your past searches. Your brain stores your every little move but puts in front of you only what you normally use. So from what you see, the mind automatically deletes quite a few things that it calculates will not be required. The mind doesn't register commonplace details too. Your eyes see and your brain processes a lot more information than your conscious mind notices. Your trained eye can notice 20,000 things in a blink. A lot of that information is pushed to the back as the mind decides that it will not be needed. That is why when you try to think hard about some person or some incident, you are able to recall some of the previously forgotten details!

You can test this right away. It is a very interesting exercise. You can try it right now. Look outside your window for 5 seconds. Close your eyes now and recall what all you had seen. If you want to, note them down. Now look outside the window again and check out what you were able to recall and what were the things that you couldn't recall, though you had seen them. You will find that the mind doesn't store everything.

The same thing happens with the auditory sense also. You play a piece of music. If it is of your liking then your ears will get tuned to it and you will enjoy it and notice all the finer nuances that you are keen on. Then let there be a piece of music that is not to your liking. Your mind will just switch it off. Even if you want to listen to it, you will not be able to because your mind will not support you. You must have experienced it more vividly in the classroom! So many times you are not able to focus on the lecture because you don't like the topic or the teacher. Relationships suffer the most because of this play. All your sensory experiences go through this trick. Whole experience gets registered in the mind. In some instances, it has come to light, that if the incident is too traumatic in any relationship, the mind refuses to accept it and doesn't register it. So, the person doesn't have any memory connected with that incident. This happens in extremely painful relationship experiences.

Then the remaining event/interaction with the person goes through another filter called Distortion. Your brain rearranges the event/meeting as per your preferences again. You have your own set of preferences. Reasons for it vary and are unique to you. Sometimes, even you are not able to explain the reason for your preference. That is why if you ask ten different witnesses about the same event, you will get ten different eyewitness accounts because everyone has a different truth, which is his/her own truth. Here you have to understand that truth has two categories. One is the universal truth, like the sun rises in the east and sets in the west. There is no dispute over it anywhere in the world. Then there is the personal truth. This is based on individual likes or dislikes, preferences, and past experiences. There are variations! Points of conflicts in relationships arise from here. Which is a better sport: cricket or football? Who was more beautiful between Aishwarya Rai and Sushmita Sen? Which music is more enjoyable: country or jazz? Which music is more hummable: old film songs or latest film songs? You will get very different answers but everyone will be speaking truthfully. Opinions are based on these beliefs, preferences, or experiences. And these differences in opinion become the first hurdle in relationships.

The third filter is Generalization. Generalization is the belief system that you develop to categorize people, their actions, and behavioural patterns. The mind uses this filter depending on its need. This filter starts getting embedded in your mind right from your childhood. Whatever you hear your elders saying, general conversations happening around you, or snippets of conversation you comprehend; your exposure to society, every experience, every conversation, every look, adds to and strengthens this filter.

For example, if, since your childhood, you are told that one should not run after money, or one should have just enough money to take care of one's needs as excess money distorts your value system, then, of course, you will grow up to have a love-hate relationship with money and rich people. You will work hard and work honestly to earn money but you will not be able to have due respect for it. When time comes to take a stand, you will not feel right for negotiating hard for your pay package. You will admire rich people but will not be able to respect them.

A very common example, almost everyone has a bias against it, is between a mother-in-law and a daughter-in-law. Every girl grows up hearing stories of harsh and ruthless mothers-in-law. Every mother brings up her son hearing stories about the selfish and lazy daughters-in-law. This bias is not only in India but I can say it is universal bias! So, when a daughter-in-law comes in her new family, she enters it with dreams about a beautiful home and future but along with those she carries loads of apprehensions about her mom-in-law. Same is the case with mother-in-law. She is also carrying this fear of losing her son to a stranger. Now, you can imagine the kind of relationship these two will have. Mostly this relationship ends up being bitter. Though most of the time both the persons involved are not mean, but their bias against each other does not allow them to see the reality of each other. A mother-in-law's bias makes her insecure about losing her son and a daughter-in-law's bias makes her insecure about losing her husband. In reality the true reason is insecurity in the relationships but it is blamed onto a person.

I would like to share one example of a friend. She is a lively and bubbly person. She has two sons. She is from North India, where the bride at the time of wedding covers her head. Her son got married to a South Indian girl where the bride doesn't cover her head. You know, in India, every caste and area has its own customs. Now, when the wedding got over as per South Indian style, and the new bride was entering her house to receive the blessings of the elders of the groom family, my friend covered the head of her daughter-in-law. At that time the daughter-in-law kept quiet but she got very upset. She complained that her mother-in-law did that deliberately and tried to cover her face and lovely hairstyle and thus spoiled the photographs! Whereas, the mother-in-law had done that to protect her new daughter-in-law from the taunts and snaps of the elders of the family. No one was at fault; because of their existing presuppositions, both gave the whole event a very different colour. They were not alone. Most of us suffer the same handicap.

So now imagine how fragile the relations are when they have to suffer this handicap all the time. Everyone has his own set of biases, different mindset and very different expectations from the relationships. It is almost a miracle that the relationships survive with so many probabilities! But they do and the healthy ones thrive because the involved parties want them to and they work towards them.

If you want your relationships to work, nurture and protect them. Provide happy, positive, and supportive memories to each other. All the relationships develop based on memories and experiences. If the memory is good and sharp, it will help you to have a better relationship. And if the experience is not good, your memory also will not be good and it will not help in developing a good relationship. These memories and experiences work as a brick in any relationship. It is not easy. But then no good thing comes easily!

You see, sometimes our perceptions create very awkward moments in life. I was on a short-term assignment in a very reputed school. The admin checked with me if I was comfortable there—I was not. So I told them very honestly and when asked for the reason I shared that no one was friends with me. Teachers were cautious of me as I had come there out of the blue. I told the admin that either I should be put through the regular line of interviews or I will leave once my short-term contract is over. So the management was very kind to give me a date and time for the formal interview. Mind you, till then I had never given any interview so I had no idea how formal interviews are conducted! My perception of an interview was a formal question-answer session between two formally dressed people. On the given date and time, I was waiting outside the office, all dressed up in formal attire. The PA indicated me to go in. I knocked, went in, said sorry and came out and sat down. After a few moments, the principal came out and asked me, 'What happened?' My answer was, 'Sorry, I had not realized that your meeting is not yet over!' She explained that those people were waiting for me as I had requested a full formal interview. You see, I had never realized that the interview was to be taken by six people! And that too for a post of a teacher! I was so excited and happy to know that these six learned people have made time for me that the first thing I did after re-entering the room was to thank them for their time. The panel was a little taken aback by my enthusiasm but during and after interview they changed their perception about me and were happy to have me on board. Two things came out of this event: Firstly, my authority in my field got established and the doubt in the mind of the staff also got cleared; secondly, I learnt not to jump to conclusions without having the details. The second lesson was the most valuable. If you really look at the whole chain of events, you will also agree that it was designed to happen. Those people had to come into my life and take it into a different direction. The friends I made there are still in my life and adding value. Any relationship based on honesty lasts longer.

Many a time you lose an opportunity to build a good relationship because you do not open your mind to it. Nothing can be a clearer example of closed mindset than this real-life story. In its heyday in music, recording studios 'Decca' was one of the biggest names. On 1 January 1962, a group of aspiring musicians from Liverpool auditioned, but Decca wasn't impressed. In the opinion of its executives, Guitar Bands had had their day, and this bunch of scruffy misfits weren't going to change that anytime soon. They couldn't even spell the word 'beetle' right. That group was, of course, The Beatles and they went on to conquer the world of music and Decca's loss was good news for the much smaller record label EMI, who gave the soon-to-be Fab Four a chance, and sat back and watched the money roll in. So, you see, things that are different or new are not necessarily bad. Now, had Decca given The Beatles a chance, the story could have been very different. But they spoiled their relationship due to their set perception of the future of the guitar music and young boys who had misspelled 'beetles'. What will you call it? The Beatles' destiny and Decca's free will? Decca couldn't see the commitment of the musicians, the freshness of the group, and their mass appeal, so they didn't give the band a chance! Had they exercised a little flexibility, the result could have been much different.

So now that we have understood the functioning of the mind, it would be easier for you to understand relationships and the way they are perceived in your mind.

In the next chapter, we will discuss how we can understand relationships and save them from misunderstandings. Most relationships turn into painful experiences only due to misunderstandings.

Chapter Four

Congruence: Within and Outside

'Intrinsic security doesn't come from what other people think of us or how they treat us...It doesn't come from our circumstances or our position. It comes from within. It comes from accurate paradigms and correct principles deep in our own mind and heart. It comes from inside-out congruence, from living a life of integrity in which our daily habits reflect our deepest values.'

~ Stephen Covey

(Stephen Richard Covey was an American educator, author, businessman and a keynote speaker)

It has been discussed in Chapter 2 that you meet many people in your lives as per your destiny, but the only thing that you have in control is how you respond to them. Here the key word is 'Response'. And your response happens as per your personality. People come and go in your life and you have no control over it. You may not agree right away but if you close the book and look around, you will realize that it is a fact.

You have many relationships, connections, acquaintances; all different from each other. Yet they are connected and the connecting thread is you. All those people know you in different capacities. Some are your family members, some are your friends, some are office colleagues or connections and they all see you in different ways. You open up your inner self as per the needs of the relationship. Everyone understands that and trusts you. It is more important that you trust yourself. To do that you should have faith in your capabilities and know yourself. This will reflect in your self-esteem, which will depend on the kind of image you carry of yourself in your mind.

Let's do one very interesting exercise. Sit in a comfortable place. Relax. Keep your shoulders straight and back erect. I will give you few simple, known words, see how you visualize them. Keep a mental note of the picture that comes to your mind when you read that word. Okay! All clear? Ready?

So the first word is - TABLE

Second word is - CHAIR

Third word is - FAN

Fourth word is - FRIEND

Fifth word is - YOU

Sixth word is- MOTHER

Now that you have the chance to visualize all the words, see how clearly you were able to visualize all of them. What kind of association does your mind have with each of them? When you visualized 'table' was it a centre table, a dining table, an office table, or a picnic table? Was it low, high, round, square, long, three-legged, or four-legged? Likewise, for every object you had multiple choices. Notice what kind of object you have visualized. The image that has come first in your mind will indicate your core connection with the object, the rest are variations of the objects. You will notice that in your own house also you pay more attention to that. For example, when you thought of 'fan', a picture of a table fan flashed in your mind. If you look back you must have shown more interest and involvement in the purchase of one!

Now let's come to people. With the word 'friend' you had similar choices; childhood friend, good friend, bad fiend, supportive friend, a friend who betrayed you, your best friend, or a friend that you had lost. You see, again, with every relation you also have multiple choices. Which one is more prominent in your mind? Now, recollect what image came to your mind when you thought of yourself. This is most important. Be honest to yourself. When you visualized yourself, what kind of image flashed in your mind? Was it clear and sharp, blurred or hazy, a single image or running images, focused or out of focus, black and white or coloured, past image or current image? Was it full length or a passport photo type? All these questions are important as they indicate how you see yourself. Do you see yourself clearly in your own mind or are you not very clear? Are you able to see your positive or negative aspects or do you see all the aspects of your personality? Are you stuck in the past or are you in the present?

 When we get into it deeper and ask the person to visualize himself in the different roles—and I have experienced this aspect also—some people see themselves very clearly in certain areas but in some areas their personal image remains blurred. Their lack of congruence will be reflected in their relationships very clearly. The roles in which they carry a clear image of themselves will have very good and strong relationships, and where they are not able to have clear visualization, they will have weaker relationships! You see it is very important to know what self-image you carry in your mind. As based on this self-image you develop your persona and behavioural patterns. This is the person you introduce to everyone consciously or subconsciously. If you are happy with the person within, you will attain that congruence. If you are not satisfied with who you are, you will try to project yourself as different person to different people and that would create confusion in your relationships. You also must have come across people who are very popular in office but do not have many personal friends, or vice versa. A person is a very good son/daughter but is not a good life-partner! The reason is that in their mind they lack clarity and hence they remain unable to develop that relationship despite all their honest intentions.

You are always a work in progress and that is acceptable. But if you keep on changing the work itself then there is no progress. It is like working on a sculpture. As long as you are sure what kind of sculpture you want from that block of stone, it is okay. But if you keep on changing the sculpture itself then apart from damaging the block of stone, you will not achieve anything. To have the congruence, you have to have the trust yourself. As long as you maintain the congruence within, there is peace and harmony around you. People around you know your values and they know what to expect from you. You are the product of your environment, belief systems, and values. Your relationships have developed a comfort level with you and they can rely on you. This can happen when you are stable and you know yourself well.

> *'Trust is congruence between what you say and what you do.'*
>
> ~ Peter Drucker

(Peter Ferdinand Drucker was an Austrian management consultant, educator, and author whose writings contributed to philosophical and practical foundations of the modern business corporations)

Another very interesting aspect of your personality is that there are two of you within you. It is the same with everyone. One is the 'Idealist You' and the other is the 'Practical You'. 'Idealist You' is developed by your society, your belief system, and your desire to be someone. 'Practical You' is the messy you that is living and handling day-to-day situations. 'Idealist You' is the persona that you present (or try to!) to the society. It is your social persona. 'Practical You' is the true you who is always striving to reach the high standards set by 'Idealist You'. There is always a tussle going on inside you because of this. The idealist inside you never sits quietly. He is always pushing you to meet its standards; always pushing you to find ways and means to do the work his way. Whereas, the practical you tends to work as per the demand of the situation and circumstances. That is when you become a strong critic of yourself and, in the process, keep on chipping away the self-confidence. That is why even after achieving 98% marks, you are not happy with your performance and continue to feel that you have not worked hard enough! You will meet such other people in your office or at home who always see the negative side of the achievement only. The 'Idealist You' doesn't allow you to bask in the glory unless things are done as per his standards. That is why some of you are unable to enjoy your achievements. You feel so not out of humility but because you keep on feeling less adequate as you do not have a healthy relationship with yourself!

Everyone has these two personas in various degrees. Most of us have it in a very benign ratio. It is called 'Formal' and 'Informal'. But some of you might have it in a more developed form. You don't mean to harm anyone or dupe any one, definitely not! But then you like to think of yourselves as a certain personality and start behaving like that. This happens when the 'Idealist You' takes over your personality completely. You try to project a bigger picture of yourself. In reality, when you are alone, or no one is watching you, you are a very different person. Just visualize now the confusion and tension this person is carrying all the time. The pressure of pretence, the pressure to maintain the image, will be killing! What impact will it have on relationships? The contacts and the relations that you have with 'Idealist You' will be different from the contacts and relationships of 'Practical You'. Your relationships will not last long and they always will be constrained and confused. As long as 'Idealistic You' and 'Practical You' are on the same page, there is congruence within you. But the moment one of them tries to overshadow the other, you lose your inner congruence and chaos comes into your life.

The confusion within you starts affecting people around you. When they are not able to trust you or rely on your commitments, they start drifting away. Just remember that every person is carrying his own load of miseries, tensions, and difficulties. No one would like to add on to those. It is a simple equation: if you are not part of the solution then you are part of the problem. And no one wants to be associated with a problem.

Human beings are a part of nature. All the rules that apply in nature are applicable to human beings too. Now, everyone is aware of eco-balancing in nature. You spoil one tiny aspect of nature and it's domino effect is felt elsewhere. When the eco-balance of nature gets disturbed, there are floods, droughts, tsunamis, global warming, pandemics, etc. For example, you use too much chemical fertilizer and the water table gets infected. Do you remember the film *Erin Brockovich* and how one company's chemical waste poisoned the air and water of the surrounding area? The people living in that area started falling seriously sick with fatal diseases. In the same way, if humans lose their internal eco-balance, we also suffer floods, droughts, and tsunamis in the form of nervousness, anxiety, emotional breakdowns, pains, allergies, or diseases. You also poison your environment.

The question arises: 'What is eco-balance in human beings?' Eco-balance, or you can call it congruence, is a balance between your thoughts, speech, and actions: your Mind, heart and soul. It sounds very simple but it is not! It holds the key to most of the problems and misunderstandings. I will repeat; ***your inner*** *congruence is the key to the congruence in your external environment.*

There are certain things that are fundamental to human fulfilment. The essence of these needs is captured in the phrase 'to live, to love, to learn, to leave a legacy'. To achieve this, you have to know yourself well. Know your strengths so that you can rely upon them and know your weaknesses to work upon them.

Being in congruence, being in a healthy relationship with yourself, is very important for every aspect of your life and most important for the success of relationships. Relations are based on communication, verbal or expressions or gestures, actions, touch between/among people. As long as your actions are congruent with your speech, your speech is congruent with your thoughts and your emotions, and your emotions with your intentions, there will be no friction in your mind. But the moment, there is a mismatch in this chain, in your mind, heart and body, friction is bound to happen.

For example, you are in love with someone and you want to marry that person but your family is not in favour of this relationship. You can't go against your family as you are and have been a good son/daughter till now. But you don't want to leave this person also as you have made certain promises to them. You want to keep your promises as they were made in full honesty. Now this situation puts you in dilemma! You don't share the truth with your family and don't tell the reality to your beloved either. You are stalling your family and not committing to your beloved as well. Everyone is angry with you and you are feeling like a victim of circumstance. All your relationships are weakening. This tussle in your desires will be impacting your peace of mind, which in turn will affect your behaviour and general demeanour. If the situation continues to be like this, very soon your working environment will also start getting affected. You might lose your cool and later regret it. You will develop anxiety or nervousness start losing your appetite; eventually, your health will suffer. Your family and your beloved will blame each other. But in reality, the blame lies on you!

You see, because your mind is not settled, you are stuck in this condition. You want something else but are doing something different, so there is chaos all around! A situation that could have been a source of pleasure and celebrations has become a source of tension. Instead of adding a beautiful relation to your life, your existing relations are in jeopardy! In this situation, no one is happy and everyone is losing their inner congruence. Now just imagine another scenario where you are able to talk frankly to your family and are able to convince them, or share the reality with your beloved friend and prepare your friend for what to expect. Even if the people involved will be sad, they will not feel cheated as you have shared your truth with complete conviction. They might even come around in time.

Our ex-President of India, Mr Abdul Kalam, puts it beautifully: 'Pizza always confuses me. It comes in square box, yet when you open it, it is round. And when you start eating it, it is a triangle! Life and people are like pizza: look different, appear different and of course, behave absolutely different.' It is a perfect analogy. In life, relationships are also like this; they look different, feel different and carry a different value in your life.

Before starting any new relationships, you must contemplate its future. How will it impact your existing environment? How will it impact your existing relationships? How will it impact you? How far you are willing to go for it? If all these questions are addressed in the beginning itself and you are able to prepare the grounds for it then, you will be able to avoid a lot of pain, chaos, and confusion later. You will not feel drowned by the demands of the relationship. A lot of times, a relationship dies because people are not clear of what they expect from it. You must understand that every relationship in your life comes with a different set of rules, different expectations, and different ways of communications. These demands of the relationship start giving you anxiety and nervousness. For example, if you are not able to attend a function that you had agreed to in office, a simple prior intimation through letter/email of regret will be enough. In a social scenario, a personal call will serve the purpose. With friends, you will have to give a reason to justify your inability. With family, the reason has to be sound and convincing enough to be excused. But for the girlfriend/boyfriend/life-partner it may not be enough until it is presented with the evidence. You see, every relationship has its own dimension and you have to respect it.

Here you cannot make justifications by claiming that perhaps those relationships were destined to be in your life for this duration only, or were destined to end like this. Relationships that come and go as per destiny may also have a similar pattern but those experiences will be rare. If you are experiencing similar results in quite a few of your relationships, then you should look into your actions (free will).

I feel like sharing one example from my life, though it is not directly related but it is quite similar. When I was very young, in class three or four, I would come home very happy and proudly announced that I had been selected to be part of three or four items in the school function. As days went by, I would be dropped, one by one, from all the items but one. I would be disappointed, even cried, as I was not able to realize that to be part of so many items I was expected to be very swift and full of stamina. But I was a delicate child. Of course, once the teacher realized that I am in more than one item, they decided among themselves to replace me. My elder brother would tease me to no end. In fact, I used to dread his teasing more than anything else and would not break the news to him for as long as I could. But as I grew older, I realized my limitations and would inform the teachers during the selection time to save myself the bother and the humiliation at the hands of my brother!

The same thing happens in relationships. Sometimes you start what you are not able to finish. You don't realize your personal limitations and, as a consequence, suffer in the end.

You can try to understand it like this: suppose you want to build a small cottage. For that you lay the foundation. While building it your needs grow and on the same foundation you start to build a bigger house. Now, because the foundation was meant to be for a small cottage, it will not be able to support the big house for long and sooner or later, with the rhythmic changes of seasons, it will start needing constant attention and repairs. The same thing happens when you try to build a strong relationship without investing enough time and emotions in it. Constant pressures and emotional outbursts can crumble relationships.

Think of the form of relationship very clearly in your mind. What kind of relationship do you want? How far are you willing to go to maintain the relationship? So many times I have come across couples where there is very little common ground left, but they have decided to continue the relationship as they are still committed to it. They have a very clear understanding of the reasons to stay together and they have accepted their situation in their minds and hearts. That has brought eco-balance in their relationship. Make sure you have love and respect for the person as love brings passion in the relationship but respect brings bonding, which is very important in a relationship that you want to maintain for life. Love changes its form as you age and mature. The passion of youth gives way to companionship in middle age and to a very close, dependable support system in old age. When you add respect to this love, life's journey becomes more bearable, bringing commitment and devotion to the relationship.

If you are a parent, decide what kind of parent-child relationship you want to develop. Do you want to be a friendly parent, a disciplinarian, or a strict parent? It is important to have the focus of the relationship clear in your mind otherwise you will never be satisfied. You just might keep on oscillating and bring up a confused child who would never be able to understand what to expect from you. Being an understanding parent is the best choice. Your child doesn't need a friend in you. He looks up to you, he seeks guidance from you, he needs support and acceptance from you when he is feeling low. What he needs from you is the total reassurance that you will understand him and he can depend on you in his time of crisis. This parent-child relationship is as strong as it is fragile. There are too many expectations attached from both the sides. So keep the door of communication open at all times and move ahead. We will talk about communication in Chapter 7 - 'Be a Part of Symphony'.

In every relationship, but more so in a parent-child relationship, you need to provide the confidence to the child that you are there to protect him, guide him and love him, regardless of the situation. The child needs that confidence that your love is not conditional. Conditional love is not conducive to a healthy relationship. If your child gets the signal that if he behaves he will get love, or if he doesn't behave in a certain manner, he will not be loved, he will learn to pretend! You reprimand the child, check him, be strict with him but never stop loving him. Yes, there will be times when you will lose it but then there will be opportunities to mend it also. It is the most beautiful relationship that takes a lot from you but then the kind of fulfilment you derive from it is also unbelievable.

The key to any happy, long-lasting and confusion-free relationship is honesty, especially within yourself. Just be who you are without any pretence. If you feel that you may lose people if they see the real you then work on yourself instead working on them. As, ultimately, the truth will come out. Keep integrity and coherence in your thoughts, speech, and actions to attract the right people in your life and enjoy happy and lasting relationships with them.

Chapter Five

Web of Connections

'There is a very deep connection among human beings. All we have to do is open our minds to it.'

~ Yanni

(The famous Greek composer)

Even before you are born, people start getting connected with you. They wait for your arrival as you have a place in everyone's mind and heart. That opens a gate to a web of connections in your life. These connections, some long term, some short term, keep on moulding your life inadvertently or deliberately.

Some relationships are obvious and always remain in front of your eyes. Some relationships are in the background and provide the support that's needed from time to time. The moment life begins, your relationships start. Even in the womb, your future relations start impacting you. Their actions, comments, and statements affect your mother, which impact her emotional state and that, in turn, impact your growth. Your mother's gynaecologist has such an important role to play in your life and yet you may never meet the person. The first touch you experience in life is not from your parents but from a total stranger, who remains a stranger: your mother's nurse on duty! How do these people come together? Is it a coincidence or predestined?

One story comes to my mind. Our driver's wife went into labour in a small town. A very, very routine occurrence! Everything was going normally when the delivering nurse realised that baby was stuck. She did whatever she could but she was losing the baby. At that time, one male gynaecologist was visiting his grandmother and, out of curiosity, was checking out the village medical facility. He heard the commotion and responded to it, immediately taking charge of the situation. Very soon, the mother had a healthy, squealing baby in her arms and the nurse was saying thanks to the Almighty. It was like a scene from a film but yet a reality in our driver's life. Now, just think about how the doctor was there at that very moment and responded in that particular way! The baby was destined to live, the mother was destined to go through the agony, the nurse was destined to suffer the helplessness, and the doctor was destined to be a saviour. Everyone involved in the same incident at the same time took away a very different experience and went through very different emotions!

Like this, in every step of your life, you keep on living through direct or indirect experiences that layer your subconscious mind with very subtle impressions. As you grow, you learn to respond. Some responses are taught to you while some come naturally to you. The latter are the responses that reflect your personality. For example, when the time comes, you are sent to school. I agree, your parents decide which school you go to but what you learn there is up to you. As per your natural inclination, you get affected by the surroundings, your fellow students, the quality of teachers, and facilities as you absorb knowledge. There are so many students in the school. If you ask all the students about the school, they will give you very different descriptions. That will be their truth, a reflection of their relationship with the school. Some students will have a grateful attitude towards coming to the school, some will be quite disappointed with school , while some will feel very comfortable there! Based on their relationships, their personalities will develop; some will form lifelong friendships there, some will try to be lost in the crowd, some will boss others around, and some will just while away their time.

Your life gets shaped by the references, or impressions, you collect. These seemingly random impressions ultimately create your belief system, which becomes your pattern for life. For example, a child falls sick. In the routine life, no one used to pay much attention to him but as he fell sick everyone was concerned for him. From his grandparents to parents and siblings, everyone was trying to keep him comfortable. The impression that the child got was that he has become important by falling sick. If he experiences similar situations for some more time, it will become his belief and his mind will store this information. As he grows up, chances are that he will suffer from psychosomatic problems more often. Like this, people go through situations and take away very different impressions as per their natural instincts. It depends on how they have connected the dots.

As you grow, your circle increases. You meet many new people outside your family. You start making friends. What guides you in selecting your friend? Most of your class was friendly, but you feel comfortable with one or two fellow students only. Why is that so? Your answer might be that your personalities matched. That also is true but they were destined to come in your life and clear the debt of karmas. Sometimes, these friendships last forever and sometimes these friendships wither away as quickly as they were formed after leaving you with a very powerful message. That message may be heart-warming or heartbreaking but it leaves a deep impression on you. Now, what you do with that message, how you handle it, depends on you.

You weave your life in the web of relationships. Your relationships become a source of happiness and sorrow, pride and pity, tears and laughter, nervousness and confidence. Some relationships become so important to you that you try to change your personality, your habits, or even value system, just to keep them in your life! Some relationships become so important to you that you get lost in it. It becomes your world. But it is not necessary that you also become the main focus in that relationship. Your every thought, every action, is keeping that relationship on your mind! You remain conscious of what that person will think or want but that person lives his or her life beyond you. I have seen this happening in parent-child relationships, between life partners, and among friends too! Unfortunately, this kind of a relationship is not good for you in the long term. This becomes a web where you feel entangled and bound. Relationships form a web, no doubt about that, but you should develop a web of support and acceptance. But, unfortunately, that is not the case always. Some relationships are so toxic that they leave a very strong mark on the personality.

It is not necessary that you will get these relationships early on in your life. Life is a school which is always open and your classes continue for you or through you. I know a warm and friendly couple who were happily settled after their retirement. They got to know of their old-time friend who had come back to the city after a long sojourn abroad. They were happy to reconnect. As luck would have it, their friend passed away, leaving his widow behind. But there was no reason to worry as the son and his family were also in the same city. The son and his family moved in with the mother to take care of her. But within three years, the situation in the family became so bad that the old couple were disturbed in the middle of night by their friend's widow, sobbing and saying that her son was beating her and stealing her money. She couldn't take it any longer. Her daughter in America was arranging a Visa for her. Out of their large heartedness and for old time's sake, the retired couple took her in. Now this couple had not realized that the constant harassment by this widowed lady's son had taken its toll on her mind. The old couple had taken her in with all the good intentions but the toxicity of that family started impacting them. Ultimately, instead of the old couple being able to give that widow a happy environment, that widow brought in so much toxicity in their home that they started feeling low in three months. The old couple realized that if it continues this way, they will fall sick. It was a tussle between their minds and hearts. Ultimately, they took the strong decision and settled the widow in an independent apartment that was safe and closer to their home. They were surprised at the positive change in their house environment!

So, you see, you can get entangled in the web at any stage in your life.

A case of a young adolescent child came to me who was very depressed. During the first session, when I was talking to him, it turned out that reason for his acute depression was a friend on whom this child had put a lot of faith and trust but that friend didn't reciprocate it. He was so depressed that he thought that his life was not worth living! That child took some time to understand that his friend also had the right to choose his friends. It was sad that he didn't pick him but that is not the end of the world. He had other friends who were ready to become his best friend. At such a young age, he learnt a big lesson: some relationships are transient. They come in your life to teach you, to help you grow, and once their purpose is served, they go away, but life carries on with or without them.

Connections keep on forming and fading. Sometimes, after a long interval, you rekindle some old connections. You decide to catch up with each other and very soon you realize that you are starting something new together. It all happens out of the blue, totally unplanned! But if you stand back and look at the situation again, you will realize that it was not totally unplanned. You were ready to start something new and were just waiting for the right opportunity. Your accidental meeting with your old acquaintance was, in fact, not chance but predestined. That is why you had met that person. It happened with me too.

At a wedding reception, I bumped into a very old neighbour of ours. We started catching up and after that, we kept in touch on and off. Both of us were working for social causes. That was the common ground. One day we, again, met somewhere and started talking and our NGO was born. Both of us were surprised at how quickly things fell in place. It was destiny.

In today's corporate language, it is called networking. What do you do in networking? You keep all your connections active and remain in their mind to capture any upcoming opportunity. If you read our Hindu scriptures, whether Ramayan or Mahabharat, you will realize that even in those times networking was valued. In good times, connections were established and when the time came, they were used. Both the wars were fought not only with the help of family but with the help of people who were there for that purpose. Their presence was predestined. For some time, we can leave the scriptures aside. If you look around in your life itself, you will be able to recollect one or two instances where help or a problem came out of nowhere, unexpectedly.

I can share an instance from my life. My son had gone to study abroad and there he got a very rare viral infection. We were totally at a loss. We rushed there to be with him and look after him. He would start recovering but the virus would come back. The doctors were also baffled. They had not seen such a case like this ever before. The extended families in India also were very concerned and started consulting pundits and astrologers. During this time, an astrologer came in contact and made a forecast that until a certain yagna was done with all the rituals at a certain place, my son would not recover. The reason predicted for his illness was, to us, quite far-fetched and unbelievable. But he was adamant. Ultimately, we did whatever he had suggested and my son started recovering. The doctors were relieved and surprised. The disease didn't relapse. Everyone in the family was duly impressed and wanted to consult this astrologer but one fine day, he just vanished, never to be seen again. Where he appeared from and vanished to is still a mystery. He came as a blessing, guided us in our difficult times, and disappeared. Like this incident, there must be others in your life too.

I firmly believe that in our lives all our major emotional experiences happen due to others. We have very little control over them. It may be securing the highest marks, getting a job, getting married, a loss in the family, or a profit in the share market; you will realize that though you are receiving the fruits, you are not the perpetrator rolling the ball into motion.

We know a family of doctors. Their daughter-in-law conceived her first child. During pregnancy, she suffered from German measles. She didn't disclose her condition and nobody noticed it either! Surprising, isn't it? But this happened and in due course of time, a healthy baby girl was delivered. Very soon it was evident that she was deaf and mute! Everyone was shocked. During the investigation it came to light that the mother had suffered from German measles. A family of renowned doctors was destined to go through the rigours of this experience, so they did. But mind you, how they go through this experience was in their hands, whether to turn it into a punishment or turn it into a learning exercise. They had their free will. They decided to follow the latter and everyone lived, learned, and laughed together. Today that girl is happily married and is a good artist.

Every step of your life, every experience, directly or indirectly, keep on layering the subconscious with very subtle impressions that mould your personality.

In this chapter, we have read about the connections and their effect on our lives. We have read that every relationship in our lives is there for a certain purpose and a certain time.

Chapter Six

Fly Light Or Bend Under Baggage

'Never limit your views of life by any past experiences.'

~ Ernest Holmes

(Ernest Shurtleff Holmes was an American New Thought writer, teacher, and leader. He started a Spiritual movement known as Religious Science, whose philosophy is known as 'The Science of Mind')

Now that it is clear how relationships come to life and how the mind perceives them, we can focus on how to develop and strengthen relationships, and how to take them forward.

Right from birth, till you die, you remain surrounded by relations in one form or other. Most of your joys and sorrows are experienced through them. Right from childhood, if you try to recollect, most of your strong memories are associated with your relationships. Somebody gave you a good present, or somebody gave a surprise visit, or somebody did not invite you to a party or somebody ignored you in the gathering; there will be innumerable memories that have made your life rich with experiences. You get them from relations and to share them also you need relations. You just can't do without them. You can say that your life is the sum total of your relationships!

When these relationships are so important in life then you must pay very close attention to them. There are some relationships that can endure a lot of pressure and still survive. It depends on the people in it and what they have experienced in the past. Obviously when you have life, you will have a past too. Every passing moment is adding to your past. In the past, if there are happy memories, there are bad ones too. But some people are not able to leave them behind. Wherever they go, these memories also go along with them. These people are not able to come out of them. They are not able to get closure they need from these incidents. Hence these incidents always remain in the present and impact their current relationships. They are like a heavy baggage that moves along with them.

You should try to give proper closure to every experience. By doing this, you mentally and emotionally accept that this incident is over and you have learnt your lesson. Every incident gives us an experience and every experience leaves us with a memory. You have to decide whether you use these experiences as a chance to learn or a platform where you are stuck. Always be aware of your emotional baggage because it impacts your relationships adversely and does not allow you to be emotionally present. For any thriving relationship, it is very important to keep it baggage free; that baggage can be of the past or expectations! A healthy relationship needs trust, breathing space, and respect.

Sometimes when one person is upset, it is advised that the other person should listen and keep quiet. This advice of 'keeping quiet' is good but keep quiet for how long? By this behaviour, you are just delaying confrontation and allowing the problem to simmer. For a baggage-free relationship, the best action in this situation is to allow the steam of other person to release and once the person has cooled down, then address the core issue, not the reaction or the tantrum. When you become quiet or ignore the problem, it irks the other person. That person will carry the grudge or the irritation for a long time and it will impact the relationship adversely.

Some parents, despite all their love and commitment to their child, suffocate the relationship with the baggage of their expectations from the child. Some good friendships wither away as they suffer from past distrust of one person. Marriages fail as one of them has brought the baggage of a previous betrayal into this relationship. Don't allow one bad experience in any relationship to overshadow your other relationships. When you are in any relationship for long term commitment, some hurdles are bound to come. You have to learn to take them in your stride.

Let's discuss parent-child relationships first. It is the most beautiful and fulfilling relationship. The moment parents become aware of the new arrival, they start planning and dreaming. Their life revolves around the unborn baby. Mothers start eating what they think will be good for the baby even if they don't like it. Fathers also become extra attentive towards their wives to provide them all the comfort possible. They look forward to holding the baby in their arms. And then the baby arrives. These people create their own world where everything revolves around each other. Everything remains fine but sometimes trouble comes when the child starts showing a personality that is different from what the parents expected. The parents, apprehensive for his future, start pouring their fears into his life.

The initial stages in a parent-child relationship are all about celebrations and fatigue! Every new activity/learning of the child is celebrated. Parents dote on their child and the child adores his parents. Both are the centre of each other's universe. As time passes, the child grows, becomes a young adult. He develops his own style of working and points of view on life. Now, this is the time for parents to be alert. If, as a parent, you have tried to impart the right value system to your child, you need not worry much. Like every other human being before him, your child will also try to push the set boundaries. This is the time to be firm, affectionate, and patient. He will fall in line.

If the child has learnt from you, his mind is clear on how he needs to conduct himself. The problem arises when the child is confused. Sometimes parents teach him all the good values, how he is expected to behave, but they themselves do not follow what they have preached. So the young mind deduces that one should be aware of the values but is free to behave as one desires! This belief creates problems. The only way to avoid this confusion is vigilant self- control in front of the child. You see, parenting is not easy.

Parents are also a product of their past and their circumstances. Their dreams and expectations may turn out to be different from their child's and that becomes a point of friction. Parents feel that they have the authority on guiding their child and the child feels that it is his life—he knows what he is doing! But both are right and wrong. Yes, parents have more experience, so they can foresee the results better, but things are different from their times. Yet the child should also respect their experience and listen to their advice as that is always valid. Parents and children share a special emotional bond. Whatever the situation is, that bond survives.

Parents and children come into each other's lives as per their destiny. What they make out of this relationship is their free will. At the beginning of his life, a child needs the support of his parents to survive and develop. Parents also leave no stone unturned to provide the best of everything within their means.

Sometimes because it is needed, and sometimes they try to fulfil their childhood desires through their child. Basically, they do everything for the happiness and safety of their child. The child also remains fully dependent on his parents for his physical, emotional, financial, and spiritual needs. As his circle increases, his social and psychological needs start getting fulfilled from outer sources.

How a child sees his parents depends on his perception. Sometimes a child also develops baggage. Parents have no control over it. If parents have more than one child, they will know that every child sees his parents in a different light as every child has a different perception. In today's world, the reality of the family situation may be very different than what it seems from outside. I know many a family who seem to be flourishing from the outside but are very different up close! How much of it the child is able to comprehend depends on his ability of observation. I know of a family of four where both the parents are working. As both of them are working, they need two cars. They have already purchased a house in a good area so a major portion of the income is going in for its monthly instalments. With both the parents out for the whole day and coming late in the evening, a full-time help is a necessity. Both the kids are in good schools. So the school fee, bus fee, uniforms, school trips, projects etc., also take away another substantial chunk of their income. Then, of course, there is the running expense for the house. At the end of the month, the couple is left with very little extra money. Surprisingly, the younger boy understands the situation but the elder boy is always cribbing and complaining. the parents thought that the elder son will be more mature and would be in better position to understand their situation, but this was not the case! He sees the outer luxuries and is not able to see his parents' hard work behind the big house and cars and the other paraphernalia.

This is not an isolated case. I have seen many households going through this dilemma. The only way to sort it out is to share the situation with your child. He might be young but he will be able to understand it if you explain it to him at his level of understanding. If you share it with him, he will also feel part of things and be more supportive. You see, not every person is perceptive but most are receptive. You share with him and he will feel part of the team. That will make him more responsible too.

Nowadays, I see parents' confusion about how to build a relationship with their own child. It is an alarming situation! What has changed in our society in the past 50 years? The strongest bonding has become so weak that once the child is an adult, his old parents are not sure of their place in his life! Let's not look outside to put the blame. Do some introspection and you will realize the reason is very much within the family itself. Instead of connecting with their child at an emotional level, they just got busy in providing the child with material things. The best brands of toys, clothes, or food items replaced quality time. Or, due to their baggage of past experiences or apprehensions, the child started seeing his parents as a resource to fulfil his demands. His cupboards and room became over stuffed but the emotional and sometimes spiritual void kept on increasing. Relationships are not based on material comforts; they are built on emotional and spiritual bonding.

I would like to say one thing: parenthood is a relationship that is the most natural. Regardless of age, status, culture, background, or religious beliefs, parenthood brings out the best in people. Parents are willing to make sacrifices willingly for their offspring. All first-time parents walk the unknown road of parenthood with nervousness yet with confidence. Their love for their child, their total and unconditional commitment to his safety, gives them the instinctive knowledge and confidence to take care of him! It is a beautiful relationship that makes the couple feel complete.

Yet this relationship has brought so much of heartache and a sense of betrayal to both parents as well as their child that it is shocking! How does such a beautiful and caring relationship become so dry and distant? One set of parents can bring up all their offspring but all the children combined are not able to take care of their parents. Why does society feel the need for old-age homes? Why do children become so disconnected with their parents that they stop having time or patience for them?

To keep any relationship alive, one has to nurture it with love and care. Parents provide aplenty to their child and that is why he is there. But sometimes, they forget to bring balance to it. Sometimes they just freeze in the time frame and continue to do what they were doing for their child when he was a baby. Or sometimes they go to the other extreme: to help the child grow up, in their desire to help him become independent, they cut off their support in a way that the child starts feeling lonely and distant with them. They do not do it deliberately. They see their friend doing it and achieving good results so they want the same for their child too. But in their involvement, they forget that everyone has a different personality and a different way of learning. What is good for one person may not be the right way for other. As the word relation itself denotes, it's all about how the person relates to you, the situation, or the idea! How have you communicated the idea to him? How has the child communicated his desire to be independent? Are both of you on the same page or not?

In the same way, the other very strong and long-term relationship is the relationship with life-partner. As you grow up, you start dreaming of a person with whom you will share your life, go through the ups and downs, and always be together and grow old with; the husband–wife relationship is the complete package. This is the only relationship in which you connect with the person at all the levels, be it emotional, mental, physical, spiritual and financial. The husband and wife depend on each other and complete each other. Here I would like to give a very sincere advice in the beginning itself: please don't assume that your partner knows everything that you expect from this relationship. No one can read your mind. You have to express/convey/speak/share your desire and views. Relationships should be based on communication, not on assumption.

I really like this line I read somewhere: 'Marriage never dies a natural death, it is always murdered; either by ego or by lack of communication.' It is so true! It is accepted across the cultures. It is like a universal truth. In a very famous novel, Yayati, written by Gyanpeeth award winner, Marathi writer Mr V. S. Khandekar and translated in Hindi by Mr Y. P. Kulkarni, the author says, 'Marriage is the most sacred undertaking where the first demand from you is to relinquish your ego.' In marriage, there is no place for ego. When there is ego in marriage, communication fails. You know what should be said and when it should be said but your ego stops you for a moment and you lose the chance. Sometimes a big and ugly situation can be averted just by taking a step back, but your ego comes in the way to ask, 'Why me?'

All this can be avoided if you just look beyond the present situation.

Marriage can survive a lot of hardships but it cannot survive a suffocating environment where there is no communication. However much you are upset with your partner, don't shut him out. Keep the communication channel open. Always be ready to listen to his side of the story too. If you come across the same excuses and similar story again and again, then sit together and sort out the reason and the cause of this behaviour. If there is a desire to be together, then working on it should be doable, even if not easy.

Communication in marriage gets adversely impacted mainly by ego and secondly by assumption. Ego not only hampers the communication, it warps it as well! People sulk in the relationship, they start speaking rudely, their expectations become unrealistic. Childlike tantrums do not help in taking the relationship forward. I have seen some marriages breaking only because one partner was not willing to accommodate the other person. His reason for doing so was his past experience or beliefs about this relationship. He just couldn't get over that bad experience and he spoiled another relationship because of it.

Remember that no two people are the same, hence no two relationships are same. If you had to go through one bad experience in a certain relationship, it doesn't mean that the next relationship will also go in the same direction. Some people remarry after a very messy divorce, and have a very fulfilling and happy second marriage. I know a friend who had gone through tremendous pain in his first marriage. Divorce left him emotionally, physically, and financially very weak. After a few years, he married again and now the couple is so happy, their children, parents, and old friends visit them for a good time.

If you let your past experiences go after learning from them, you will feel enriched. If you hold on to your past experiences, then you will be burdened by them. These relationships come in your life to settle your karmic accounts. You settle them and close the chapter. Because of them don't open a new karmic account. Please don't create a chain! Appreciation and expression go a long way in every relationship, more so in a marriage. This is the most important relationship of life. You develop this relationship in your adult life. This is the only relationship that offers fulfilment at all levels, be it physical, social, mental, emotional, intellectual or spiritual. You get your partner as your destiny dictates but you build the relationship with free will. So be attentive and alert to its needs.

This relationship becomes your base from which you function. You build your home together where you dream to find love, laughter, understanding, and security. You dream your future together. You are supposed to function as a single unit and you aspire for just that. To achieve that you should bring transparency between each other. There should not be secrets. There should be trust. There should be faith that the vulnerability of one will not be exploited by the other. The list is long and might need another book!

Now we can discuss office relationships too. These relationships also play a very important role in your life and impact your family life too. In this relationship, you learn from every one and gain more experience. This relationship also is somewhat like a marriage! The moment you sign on the dotted line, you get your mentors, leaders, colleagues, juniors, support staff and of course, your HR department to rely upon. The beauty is that you are expected to prove your worth almost immediately, though on paper you get some settling time.

Office relationships impact you on more than one front. They not only impact you emotionally but they affect you at a very personal level. You start associating your personal worth as well with them. Gone are the times when the person used to retire from the organization that he had started his career from. Now, people use jobs as a stepping stone for their career. In the process you change many jobs.

In every organization you come across different characters and gain different experiences. You go through some good experiences and some not so good ones. But that doesn't stop you from looking for another job. In an office situation, you always hope for the best. You go through some apprehensions but don't carry the baggage. Because if you had, you would not have been able to change the job!

So many people associate their personal worth with the position they hold. It is a very dangerous association. Job security is never guaranteed! Just imagine the consequences of a sudden job loss. So many confident, assertive, and authoritarian people feel totally lost after their retirement. They have the same capabilities, the same personality, they had before retirement, but they feel not only stripped of authority but of their skills and personality because they are no longer holding the same position. This is the result of a misguided relationship with their job title.

So, to sum up this chapter, I would like to reiterate that don't allow your past experience of relationships drag you down. Learn from them and make them into stepping stones instead of a pebble in the shoe.

Chapter Seven

Be A Part of Symphony

'To effectively communicate, we must realize that we are all different in the way we perceive the world and use this understanding as a guide to our communication with others.'

~ Anthony Robins

(Anthony Jay Robins is an American author, coach, and is known for his Webinars and self-help books)

The world is connected through vibrations and sound waves. Animals communicate through sounds, signs, and body language. Humans are also blessed to have words, expressions, and tones. We have fully developed the art of communication!

Human relations are based on communication and needs. Out of the two, communication forms a stronger basis for relationship. When communication is so important, you would have thought that all humans would be master of it! But sadly, that is not the case. The thread that brings people together quite often becomes the reason for the entanglement in their relationships as people are not paying attention to communication.

'Any Problem, big or small, within a family, always seems to start with bad communication. Someone isn't listening.'

~ Emma Thompson

(Emma Thompson is a British actress, screen writer, producer, activist, author and comedian)

Communication is the oxygen for a relationship. All relations are based on it. Without this, the relationship cannot survive. Words play a major role in it but listening to those words is more important! What is being tried to convey through those words? What is the intention? What is the reason? Mostly people don't go past beyond the words. Once a colleague of mine was speaking to her young teenage daughter about how she was leading a tension-free life whereas my colleague, her mother, could not have a second of rest. The daughter just uttered one word: 'Really?' And that word was loaded! But my colleague was so involved in herself that she didn't hear what her daughter had really said. In my colleague's eyes, her daughter had agreed with her. She heard what she wanted to hear, not what was being tried to convey. Remember the rule 7-38-55 of Albert Meherbian. It says that in communication, the words communicate 7%, your tone conveys 38%, and your body language conveys 55% of the meaning of your communication.

So if you really want to listen, pay attention to the tone and the body language along with the words.

Communication is not a monologue; it is inclusive of all the parties involved. If we want to have a healthy relationship, then communication should be like a symphony where each instrument is adding to the richness of the sound and has its own place. If that is not the case, then there is imbalance in it and it might turn into cacophony. To have healthy relationships and a healthy environment, every family member should listen to each other. Families thrive when there is more communication and fewer announcements.

While communicating, we should realize that the responses we get are the results of what we communicate. Communication is not only what you speak but what you hear as well! Speaking and listening, both are equally important in the art of communication. In fact, I would say that in relationships listening is more important than speaking! If you are a good listener, you will understand the other person better and will be able to come up with a more appropriate solution/advice/suggestion/responses.

For a healthy relationship, communication is not an exchange of information. It is an exchange of thoughts, ideas, dreams or intentions. In today's world, where everyone is busy and running short on time, sitting face to face and exchanging information is also a luxury! Children grow up and become adults without knowing the person in their parents. Couples also lose touch with the person whom they had married. It is sad but it is a fact. That is why relationships have become so fragile now.

I remember when my husband took his charge in Cairo, Egypt; it was Ramadan time there. Office time was from 9.30am to 2.30pm. So he used to come home around lunch time. As we had just reached there, I was also not working. Whereas in India, both of us were working. Mornings were always hectic as I was working in school so I used to leave early, and he, being in the corporate world, used to come home late in the evening. So we would all sit together at the dining table, exchange the news and day's proceedings with each other, and retire for the day. Now here in Cairo, he would be home so early! It started putting pressure on me and my son. Till then, we always had more to share with him than we had the time. But now we had so much time and we did not have anything to tell him! This was a new situation for us. I realized that we had lost the comforting habit of sitting and sharing the silence. Due to our hectic schedules, all three of us were mostly exchanging information or instructions. We relearned to communicate and get comfortable staying silent! It was a very important and most cherished gift that Cairo gave me.

A lot of time in relationships, both the parties are so keen on expressing themselves that they just keep on presenting their points of view and don't listen to what the other person is saying. Both get upset that the other person doesn't listen, but do they? You just expect that other person should listen to you. All the expectations are from other person! What about you? Are you listening? If the other person is making a mistake of not listening to you then are you also not guilty of doing the same? The biggest problem is that most of the time you don't listen to understand, you listen to reply. It is more important to understand the person than forming the perfect response! If you want the relationship to develop, survive, and thrive, then you have to develop the art of listening.

Yes, listening is an art! It is a skill that needs to be developed. You must have come across people who understand what you are trying to say or how you are feeling without being told and left you wondering, 'How did they do it?' God has given us ears to hear but listening is more than that. You hear sounds. But you listen to the person. When anyone speaks, it is not only words. Those words are rolled in tones and expressions, expressed through body language and pauses, controlled with speed and volume. Sometimes no words are spoken and still a person is able to convey a lot. Sometimes silence is louder than words. Who can understand it better than the family member who has crossed the 'night out' curfew?

Have you ever had a chance to interact with a deaf and mute person? My cousin sister is one. Her husband is also deaf and partially mute. Their interactions are so beautiful and detailed without uttering a single word! Their arguments can also get quite intense. Observing them made me realize that words play a very small role in communication. It is mostly your gestures, expressions, and emotions that hold the key.

If you just pay attention to the spoken word then chances are that you have missed out at least 50% of what was communicated. Remember the very popular punctuation phrase: 'Come on now, go! We will see later.' If you change the place of comma, it goes: 'Come on, now go, we will see later.' You see, pauses also play a very important role during communication.

So when you are asked to listen in any relationship, please pay attention to the body language, volume, expressions, breathing pattern and everything. Body language will convey the comfort anxiety or nervousness levels of the person. You will be able to gauge the person's mental and emotional state. If need be, you may be able to calm the person before listening to the whole story, and in the process, you may be able to save your energy and the situation both.

There are different people and different ways of communicating. As we have already read in Chapter 3, 'Mosaic of Memories and Perception', everyone has a different way of perceiving the same way we have different ways of communicating. Everyone's mind is wired differently. What works for one person may not work for the next person. What appeals to you may not appeal to your sister, though both of you have been brought up by the same parents in the same environment. So many times, I have heard couples telling me that the partner doesn't listen. Not listening to each other is the main problem. Why does it happen? It is not that they want to ignore each other but it is just that the mind doesn't connect. The husband will bring flowers, birthday cards, gifts but the wife feels that he doesn't love her. Or the wife keeps on preparing lovely meals, or expressing her love for him, but he feels that she doesn't love him! This is happening in their life not because they have stopped loving each other but due to their inability to engage their partner's mind while expressing themselves.

To solve this mystery, there is a solution. Psychologists have researched and found out that there are three kinds of listeners:

1. Visual Listeners

2. Auditory Listeners

3. Kinaesthetic listeners

VISUAL LISTENER: 65% of the human population falls in this category. They are the ones whose minds get involved easily with the visuals. If you want to grab their attention, use words like show, look, see, visualize, illustrate, vision. They will always express their love through lovely visuals. They would love to go to beautiful locations for holidays. They would always like to wear beautiful and colour-coordinated dresses and would like to receive and gift beautiful things that are prettily wrapped. They would be more artistic and creatively inclined. They would like to watch instead of listening. Use descriptive words with them. Show them that you love them. They notices gestures. Words or display of feelings matter but gestures are more important. Another cue is that visual communicators tend to talk a little faster as they tend to verbalize the picture that is running in front of their eyes. When they recall anything, they look up towards the right, and when they are planning, they look up towards their left.

AUDITORY LISTENER: 30% of people belong to this category. People from this category will always respond to words like listen, hear me out, talk, lets sort it out, lets chit-chat, amplify, I am telling you, etc. They would like and enjoy discussions more than an outing or a film. To them, verbal expression of feelings is more important than all the gifts you give. Verbal reassurance is more important than actions! On the cautious side, as they are auditory inclined, they remember all the conversations and can dig out old quotes, even old conversations! Tell them that you love them. A clue to know that the person is auditory is that they choose their words very carefully. When interacting, they tend to bend forward, or come to the edge of their seat. When they try to recall, they look sideways towards their right and when thinking they look sideways towards their left.

KINEASTHETIC LISTENER: Only 5% of people are from this category. People belonging to this category can be complex listeners. Mostly they are energetic and like to keep themselves busy with different hands-on activities. They loves to experiment. This person will always listen to words like feel, experience, touch, roughly, relaxed, swell, smooth, etc. They will value a hug more than any expensive gift. For them, feelings are more important than any gift. Make them feel that you love them. A clue to recognizing them is that they tend to take pauses during their conversations as they tend to feel the words. During conversations they tend to hold or constantly touch themselves or some object. You must have noticed some people playing with a pen or pencil all the time while talking. When they try to recall things, they tend to look downwards to their right and when they are thinking they tend to look downwards towards their left.

Sometimes it is most difficult to communicate with the person who is closest to you. You can face this situation as a friend, sister, daughter, or a wife. Sometimes, you don't want to share the negative developments with your near and dear ones. It may be because you want to protect them from hurt or you don't want to face their negative reactions. You may be right in your mind, but your family may perceive it in a different way! Remember that they are the ones who will be equally affected by it because, for one, they love you. And secondly, being a part of your life, their lives also will be impacted. It is always advisable to maintain transparency in your relationships. If any tough news has to be broken, it is best that your family hears it from you, not from outsiders. You know your family well. The way you understand each one of them, no one else does. The fact remains that by delaying or keeping quiet you don't help anyone, least of all yourself! If you have to share your misfortune with them, understandably, there will some element of embarrassment, shame, or hesitation. It will not be easy. But you will not achieve anything by postponing it either. What helps is the honesty and integrity with which you share the news to them.

Speak from your heart, where only understanding is needed. Here if you speak from your mind, it may lead to an argument as the mind uses logic and analysis. Breaking a bad news might be tough on you but it will help build trust in the family. Families come together to celebrate but they get united when faced with adversities.

Always remember that among close relationships, there is always a history. Sometimes you make a simple statement but it is taken out of context and the whole conversation takes a totally unexpected turn. And you are left wondering where you went wrong? You see, in personal communication, you are carrying a history with the person. You both know each other very well! So many times, it happens that you have made a fresh statement but your partner is still stuck in the previous conversation. Because your partner's mind is still there, your statement, for him, is the continuation of that conversation only. It is always advisable to bring in the context of the new topic and ensure that the other person has broken off the earlier subject. This will improve the quality of communication.

Anthony Robin says that people communicate as per their perception; every man has a different perception of the same situation. Everyone perceives the situation, the behaviour of other person, on the basis of his beliefs, personality, his environment, and his expectations from that person and situation and the relation! This expectation also keeps on changing with the changing situations. It is a very complex world. If you are at home, you will communicate in a certain way which will be different when you are with your friends, and, again, that will change when you are in office or in any official gathering! Now imagine everyone going through similar changes.

What complicates the matter further is the mental state of the person in these situations.

Communication is not only verbal. Your body language, your expressions, your tone also play a major part in communication. These aspects of communication convey a lot about your personality, character, and background. So use them carefully. Like a person from the armed forces background can easily be noticed by his walk and his body posture. The same way a teacher can be noticed by his body language and tone. But when we use these in communication, it takes on a different meaning.

Remember, there is a way of speaking and then there is who is speaking. Every person has a style and personality that is attached to their way of speaking. In my family, my own father was a little short tempered but very affectionate. Sometimes he would get upset if he saw us doing something where he thought we would get hurt. We had accepted that. If anyone was late by 15 minutes, Papa would worry. And out of that worry he would scold us. Everyone knew his nature and took his scolding in stride. On the other hand, my mother was very calm. So if Mummy would even look at the person with questioning eyes, it would be like a very bad reprimand. I don't remember my mother ever raising her voice. So if Mummy used to tell anyone to behave, that person would stay alert for at least a week.

In any communication, there are three points to pay attention to:

What to communicate?

What to communicate depends on the person's perception. Obviously, you will communicate the way you have perceived the situation and the opinion that you have formed on the basis of your perception. What you are speaking is your side of story.

While you are communicating, you should pay attention to the person opposite you. What is his frame of mind? Many times, problems start in relationships when you are very keen to say what is on your mind and don't pay attention to the mental or emotion condition of the other person. In this situation, whatever is communicated doesn't get received properly. Like you have perceived the situation your way, the other person also does the same. The outcome of such communication adds to the confusion and misunderstandings.

The best way to avoid any confusion is to convey the point and factual details. you can add your details and views if asked for.

How to communicate?

Everyone has their unique style of conveying the message. There are some people who are very good communicators, and we don't have to worry about them. There are people who just cannot communicate—there is no point in worrying about them. But majority of people are mix of both! You should always remember that the best time to communicate is when a person is calm and receptive. Agitation is not conducive for good communication. Keep in mind that you cannot see any reflection in churning waters. In the same way, you cannot find the solution with a troubled mind.

When there is trust in a relationship, then it is easy to communicate. When there is lack of trust in the relationship, communication becomes difficult. Because of a lack of trust, the person starts looking for a hidden motive even if there is none. The best way to communicate in this situation is to keep inflection in your tone to the minimum. Remain serious and stick to the facts. Don't present your opinion on the matter until asked for.

When to communicate?

Obviously when the time is right! But then how does one know that? The time factor depends on the information and your relationship status. I have learnt from my experience that real time transfer of information is best. By delaying the information, you cannot protect the person, you just delay the reaction and increase potential for hurt feelings.

So many times, while talking about other people, you tend to make very generalized statements like 'Oh! This fellow is always talking very loudly!' When questioned politely 'Always?' You immediately rectify your statement, 'No, not always but mostly.' It might be a simple exaggeration for you but for your mind it is big categorization! So avoid such exaggerations. I have seen it done for mothers-in-law many times. I have also been guilty of doing it. But I checked myself and dropped this habit. By pulling the other person down, you cannot lift yourself up! It is an illusion. While speaking about someone behind their back, you should be more cautious. These generalized statements don't do any good for your relationship.

To sum this chapter, I would like to say that between stimulus and reaction, there is always a space. Depending on your attitude, you can be there to use it.

Between the stimulus and reaction, there is always a space. Depending on your attitude, you can be there to use it.

Chapter Eight

Your Personal Looking Glass

'Changing your attitude from self- centeredness to understanding requires desire and commitment to always try to see things from other person's point of view.'

~ John C. Maxwell

(John Calvin Maxwell is an American author, speaker, and pastor who has written many books primarily focusing on leadership)

Till now we have discussed free will, destiny, memories, perception, connections, attitude, and communication in relationships. Now we will discuss another very important aspect of relationship: Point of view. Point of view plays a very important role in relationships as you respond to the situation on the basis of your perspective.

Your point of view is based on two things: your perception of the situation and the connection you have with the person/situation. You already know how you perceive any situation or how you form an impression of any person. On the basis of your perception of the situation/circumstances and the people involved, your own personality, and your belief system, you create your point of view. You remember the example of the North Indian mom-in-law and South Indian daughter-in-law in Chapter 3, right?

In relationships, point of view plays a very important role. People come together or drift away because of it. You know that relationships are based on communication and communication is based on the point of view. When you are willing to look at the situation from the other person's point of view, you will have a stronger relationship. But if you are not willing to even consider it then the relationship has very little chance of being a happy relationship.

We have a family of four members living in our neighbourhood. Recently, the husband lost his father. His mother is also old, but quite independent by nature, and financially too. By God's grace she is quite healthy for her age. She continues to live independently in her house in a different city. Now the family wants her to move in with them so they can take care of her in case she needs help. They would have to rush to the other city for the ailing father when he was alive. But the mother feels more comfortable in her home and wants to continue to live there and expects the family to continue making those periodic visits. The family is in a fix. They came to me to ask for my opinion. I also couldn't provide any solution except for them to sit together and sort it out together. I can see and appreciate both the points of views. But for a happy relationship, both the parties have to understand each other's points of view and find a solution.

Relationships can only survive if you are willing to see the other person's point of view and reach for a middle ground, if required. You become willing to adjust to and accommodate the other person's point of view as well. By doing so, you not only avoid friction but you support your inner growth as well.

So many people live their full life looking at the world with their tunnel view. Do you think that they have lived really? In reality, they have just passed their time on this earth living in a very small corner in their cocoon. Reaching for a compromise is not a wrong thing. It acts as a bridge in the relationships. It does not lower your self-esteem. Do not allow your ego to play with your mind. When you learn to broaden your mindset, you learn to see other points of view, and then finding a middle ground is not difficult! You will do it willingly if you value the relationship.

Your point of view comes from two angles: the connection you have with the person and your own personality. You must have seen parents picking a fight on behalf of their children on very minor issues. But in their point of view, it is not minor. In their minds, it is either for the rights of their child, or the right value-based argument, or they simply change places with their child due to their belief that the child is their extension. So the child becomes their alter ego. And, secondly, it is their point of view that their child should get his due and their misplaced belief that he can never do anything wrong. Or if by chance, some mistake has been committed, no one has the right to reprimand him except them.

It is common to see this difference in the case of love marriages. Very recently, I came across such a case. A boy and a girl decided to marry with the blessings of their parents after 6 years of friendship. Both sets of parents were aware of their friendship as they had never hidden it from anyone. So, when they decided to formalize the relationship, they did not foresee any problem. But here they were wrong! The boy's parents didn't approve of marriage as the girl was from different caste! The boy was taken aback; he tried his level best to convince his parents but they didn't agree. Both felt betrayed. From the son's point of view, his parents had betrayed his trust as they didn't object to the friendship and were always affectionate towards his girlfriend. The parents felt their trust was betrayed by the boy as they always kept quiet about his girlfriends, presuming that for marriage, he would value their sentiments and understand their point of view. In the process, they drifted apart. The son married his girlfriend without the blessings of his parents.

If only they tried to look at the situation from each other's points of view, they could have saved their relationship and expanded their family with this new relationship.

I will share with you an example from my life. I was a consultant in a big publication house. My father had passed away after suffering for almost 3 months. I was relieved and upset at the same time; relieved that his suffering was over and upset for my loss. On the day of his 'Prayer Meeting', I received a call from my office that I am required in the office. The reason given was a meeting with the managing director as he wanted to meet me. I requested them that as I am out of city and it would not be possible for me to reach in time for the meeting as it was clashing with the time of the prayer meeting. They didn't agree and persisted. I didn't go and that created a rift in the relationship. Both of us felt betrayed and refused to understand each other's points of view. I expected them to understand my situation, that I couldn't leave the prayer meeting, and the office thought that since my father was no more, it would not matter to him whether I was there at the prayer meeting or not. For them, I defied their command to keep my social image of a dutiful daughter!

This is not an isolated case, especially in the office scenario. I have seen people going back to office after cremating their loved ones! What is the relationship that the organization is nurturing if it cannot commiserate with the emotional state of its employees? Of course, such organizations do not enjoy loyalty among its employees. People work there because of the high salary and knowing this company feels that they have bought the soul of the employee. It becomes a very toxic relationship where the only connection point is 'meeting the target'; for the employer it is meeting all the deadlines and keeping the company profiting, and for the employee it is pocketing the pay cheque at the end of the month to meet their family's requirements.

How can I not talk about married couples? This topic creates the most chaos in this beautiful relationship. Most irreconcilable differences crop up only because of the inability to understand and appreciate each other's points of view. If only they allow their ego to take a back seat and allow their common sense to prevail, a lot of misery and heartache can be avoided.

Like when the husband comes home from office, he is dead tired from non- stop meetings, discussions, boss's tensions, customers' complaints and what not! He is just looking forward to some peace and quiet and a friendly cup of tea. Not too much to ask for, you will agree. The wife has also been running around whole day, getting the house in order, preparing all the meals, looking after the baby, nursing, changing diapers and taking care of his sleeping cycles. She is also exhausted and looking forward to some peace and quiet and a friendly cup of tea. Both of them are looking forward to the same scene but not together. Obviously, the scene is set for a clash.

If only they can be as patient with each other too as they were with others, the result can be beautiful. But, unfortunately, you don't have patience for the people who are closest to you. You expect them to understand you all the time. But do you also understand them all the time? Why do you assume that your partner will understand your day just by looking at your face? Maybe he is so tired that he has eyes only for the comfort of his favourite side of bed! The same applies to the husband too. Try to understand the point of view of the other person. If you want your relationship to survive and thrive, you have to learn to be patient.

I would like to help you to be able to understand other people's points of view. For this, let us do one exercise. This is a very simple yet effective exercise on understanding others' points of view.

Take three chairs. Put two chairs at the distance of at least 2 feet apart and the third chair put at some distance facing the other two chairs. Now visualize the situation that you have experienced on the difference of point of view. Please visualize all the participants too. You have already placed chairs for them. If there are more, you can increase the number of chairs but I would suggest keeping it less initially. Now sit on the chair number one. That is you. Present your views in your mind. Once you have done that properly and you have nothing more to add, give yourself a minute to calm down. Then go and sit on the second chair.

Sit on it and start thinking like the other person. Take into consideration why that person has that point of view. Once you try, you will understand the reasons that are prompting that person to behave in that manner. It may be the background, past experiences, or some other cause. Think of all the logical arguments that the person had presented. Again, take a minute to calm yourself down and shift to the third chair. This chair is facing the other two chairs. It is the chair of the observer. Now, you have seen and heard both the parties, you have observed them objectively. So take an honest decision and act on it. Chances are that you will have a more open frame of mind and will be able to sort out the situation in a much better way.

I am giving you one more tool that will help you in understanding others' points of view and will help you in your relationship.

There is another way of understanding any person and that is through his responses and personality. We must understand that the personality is the extension of a person's point of view. It has been established by a renowned psychologist Mr William Moulton Marston that people can be divided into four categories based on their personality traits: **Dominance, Influential, Steady,** and **Compliance.**

In a relationship, the dominant person will always like to be in charge of every situation, whether it is deciding the destination of holidays or ordering food,selecting curtains of the house or the school/college of children. Such a person would feel more comfortable when he is in a commanding position. Such people are the go-getters and don't hesitate in taking bold decisions. They mean well but in their pursuit of success they can become a little insensitive.

An influential person is very enthusiastic. In a relationship also he will like to do things his way but only after convincing others about it. Such a person is good at keeping relationships as he is charming, sociable, optimistic, and talkative. He uses his traits to influence others. Such a person is afraid of social rejection or being ignored, hence he doesn't mind compromising just to remain in the main team.

A compliant person adheres to the norms. He will live his life by the rules mostly set and accepted by society. He likes to be accurate and is very stable in his thoughts and actions. He is quality conscious. So he would always like to give or receive quality gifts even if they are small. If he wants to go out and eat, he would like to go to a good place. This person will look at the situation or problem from all the angles before taking any decision. Mostly such people are reserved or introverted by temperament. A person like him will speak less but notice all.

A steady person will be balanced in his approach. He will extend his support if the situation demands it. He would like to have good relationships and will maintain them too. He would like to cooperate and will try to solve the problem. He will not hesitate to appreciate others if it is due. He will keep relationships above his ego. He will be a good listener, humble, and a calm person. But the drawback can be that he can be indecisive and overly accommodating.

All of us are a combination of all the above-mentioned traits. But out of these, one trait is always predominant. In relationships, these personality traits play a very important role. The points of view are developed not only on the basis of past experiences and references but on strong personality traits too. These traits drive the person to behave and react in any given situation in a certain way. If you understand the personality, then it becomes easier to develop the relationship as you are better prepared to handle the person and your relationship with him.

Point of view can depend on the mental state of the person too. Mental state always plays an important role in relationship. Hence repetition of the advice given in the chapter 7 ' Be the part of Symphony'.

Chapter Nine

Sum Total of Relationships

So now we have come to the conclusion of the book. In this book, I have tried to look at relationships from different angles. In Chapter One, we discussed the impact of free will on our relationships. How, through our free will, we send signals through our thoughts in the universe and take our own decisions, yet achieve different results.

We have discussed the play of destiny in our relationships in Chapter Two. I believe that in life, we get what we are destined to. The only thing in our hand is how to handle the situation that we are put into. None of us had ever envisaged this lockdown situation. It was just thrust upon us. The only thing that we had in our control was our response to it. Some of us reacted in desperation and frustration, and others maintained their calm in the turmoil and sailed through it.

In the third chapter, we discussed 'Perceptions': the basis for our intention, thoughts, and actions. It is the most important as perception is the basis of our relationships and our decisions in relationships. Perceptions give direction and the strength to our relationships. They help us to build our belief system.

Perception is nothing but our personal reception of any and every situation.

In the fourth chapter, we covered congruence. Our inner congruence is very important. It helps develop our personality, self-esteem, and self-worth. Our inner congruence, along with our self-esteem and self-worth, affects our relationships not only with others but with ourselves too. We can give others only what we have! If we have love, understanding, peace and harmony, we will give that. If we have confusion, irritation, anger, and complexes, we will give that. So, in this chapter, we focused on understanding ourselves first.

The fifth chapter talks about a web of connections. We all are connected invisibly. This whole world is a big domino board. Some action takes place somewhere and the ripple effect is felt somewhere else. A person decides to build a factory, gets the land approval in some other state, and the fate of people living around that factory changes. Or the government raises some objections with the working practices of that person and asks to close the factory. The disagreement is between a person and the government but the impact is felt by the people who were not at all involved in that practice.

The sixth chapter is about how our past perception can weigh down our growth in any relationship. Past baggage can spoil any new relationship hence it is important to learn your lessons from them and leave the incident behind.

The seventh chapter is all about communication. What is the importance of communication in relationships? How can we communicate effectively and how important it is for us to develop the art of listening if we want to have healthy relationships? Then the different kinds of listeners are mentioned and the ways to connect or communicate with them effectively.

The eighth chapter is about point of view. It plays a very important part in relationships, generating the intention behind what motivates us to take action. All our conversations are based on our points of view. So it is important to understand and respect the other person's point of view, too, if we want to save our relationship and also want it to grow in a healthy manner.

In this book, I have shared my learnings from my life. I have gone through some tough situations that almost pushed me to the brink of a breakdown, where I had to do a lot of self-introspection and weigh my priorities. If, through this book, anyone can learn and save oneself from similar difficult times, then I will consider it worth the effort.

Thank you for being with me throughout this book.

www.ingramcontent.com/pod-product-compliance
Lightning Source LLC
LaVergne TN
LVHW041700190726
843493LV00007B/1880